A PREACHING WO

DAVID DAY

A PREACHING
WORKBOOK

Originally published in Great Britain in 1998
by Lynx Communications, an imprint of SPCK

Society for Promoting Christian Knowledge
36 Causton Street
London SW1P 4ST
www.spckpublishing.co.uk

Reprinted three times
Reissued as an SPCK paperback 2004

British Library Cataloguing-in-Publication Data
A catalogue record for this book is available from the British Library

ISBN 978-0-281-05732-0

Typeset by Action Publishing Technology Limited, Gloucester
First printed in Great Britain by Ashford Colour Press
Subsequently digitally printed in Great Britain

Produced on paper from sustainable forests

Contents

Foreword

'Wow' is a frequent expression when I get excited in preaching. When I can say it of someone's sermon, it is wonderful. But when people emerge from a seminar on preaching saying it, that is a terrific tribute to the teacher; and it is frequently said when David Day is the teacher.

If you have missed the seminars, you can now read the book. Of course, it hasn't the smile, the voice inflection and living example of what he is teaching, but it is the next best thing. Look at the chapter headings and you get the flavour. I soon gave up noting the arresting phrases and quotes. It is printed in black and white, but is very much in colour!

For the new preacher this book needs frequent reading and applying. For the person a few years into preaching it leads confidently back to square one to look again at preached sermons with a discerning eye. For the long-term preacher there is plenty to cheer about, to say 'yes', that's right, and how we agree that it is the passage that needs to be thought over, dug into, opened up, but it also blows us open into areas and angles that have never crossed the mind.

To be made to see how comedians communicate, to be asked sharp questions about shape and style, to be encouraged to sit around the church hearing with all sorts of different people in the one congregation, to see the value of journey and story, to face the challenge of preaching to those who usually zap from channel to channel is encouragingly disturbing!

Preaching is an awesome responsibility; the pulpit is an exposed place. We preach in the sight of our Lord; we dare not abuse the pulpit by carelessness of word and presentation. The comment 'three minutes of this and most of us have lost the will to live' means unfaithfulness in the preparation. David Day shows us, with encouragement and warning, how to be faithful to our Lord's calling. We pray, we think, we ponder, we wrestle, we apply and 'hear' and still we climb the pulpit steps, like Spurgeon, saying 'I believe in the Holy Spirit'.

Study this book and your preaching will never be the same. My sermon for next Sunday is already under redraft. At the end of the book I expect you may say 'Wow', but, even better, after your next sermon, may there be those who say 'Wow'!

Michael Baughen
Formerly Bishop of Chester

Preface

This book is intended to be a workbook. This means that you, dear reader, will regularly be invited to respond to my questions, react to my fads and analyse my sermons. From time to time I will ask you to engage with the sermons of other preachers, and even to scrutinize your own. Alas, my confidence that you will co-operate is dented somewhat by the knowledge of how I treat workbooks – from computer manuals to exercises in contemplative prayer. Working on the principle, 'If all else fails read the instructions', I skim and skip, dip and dabble, only slightly disconcerted by my failure to 'print multiple mailings from an existing data file', or stay focused for longer than three seconds. Still, like a signpost, I can point you in what I believe to be the right direction – even if I'm not too good at going that way myself.

I do strongly believe in the workbook format as far as preaching is concerned. The idea, 'This is my sermon and don't you dare touch a word of it', kills the possibility of improvement and makes sermon preparation a lonelier business than it need be. There are ninety-three-and-a-half different ways of preaching. We can all gain something from talking to each other. And in my experience, sermon workshops, with anything from four to sixty participants, have invariably been enjoyable and stimulating. Anything that encourages feedback, experimentation, disagreement, variety, fellowship and cross-fertilization can't be bad. So, as far as this book is concerned, you don't have to agree with anything I've written – but I would dearly like you to engage with it, especially the more pompous and dogmatic utterances.

Naturally, there are omissions, some of which may strike you as odd. The book contains nothing on preaching at baptisms, weddings or funerals, nothing on children's addresses, youth services or evangelistic events. I have tried to cover the sort of preaching which goes on, Sunday by Sunday, week in week out, up and down the country.

This is the basic sermon and it represents the staple diet of most congregations, of whatever denomination.

I cannot hope entirely to have avoided a denominational flavour – though in the last twelve months I have run workshops for Methodist, Baptist and Brethren preachers, who have kept me properly mindful of free-church sensibilities. Nevertheless, it would be a miracle if no Anglican assumptions had leaked in – and in one respect, at least, the material does reflect Anglican practice. When I first started to plan the book I asked clergy in the diocese of Durham if they would be prepared to let me have a copy of a recent sermon for reference. To my amazement about 50 responded – a gesture of generosity for which I am profoundly grateful. That collection of sermons has directly affected the shape and substance of the book, and has provided me with many illustrations.

There are many others whose help deserves acknowledgement. Though they are unaware of it, my debt to David Buttrick and Fred Craddock, high priests of homiletics in the USA, is obvious. I have tried to acknowledge it at every point, but I fear that much of what I have gained from their writings has now entered the bloodstream. My sincerest thanks go to all those (literally dozens) who read the text, ticking what they liked and marking the boring bits with 'zzz'; to the students at Cranmer Hall who endured early versions with fortitude and good humour; and to the undergraduate who confided that she listened to a tape of one of my sermons in order to help her get to sleep. A special word of thanks should go to Dr Walter Moberly and the Venerable John Pritchard, both of whom, independently and at a critical moment, told me in their own characteristic ways, to 'stop whingeing and get on and write the blessed thing'. Finally, I should like to thank my wife who, on too many occasions, has been driven to seek solace in her garden when she had every right to expect it from me.

Durham, 26 July 1997

Introduction

A MORON SPEAKS TO MUTES

Preaching is 'a monotonous monologue by a moron to mutes', according to R. E. O. White. This is really not a promising way to begin.

Nevertheless, everyone knows that sermons are boring. In the 1970s Bernice Martin and Ronald Pluck carried out in-depth research on the beliefs of adolescents. On one thing all teenagers were agreed, even those who never went to church: 'Sermons are boring'. As the authors said, 'This conclusion could be underlined three times'.

It's rare to find such agreement in religious matters – yet the unanimity is phenomenal. Sermons constitute an almost unendurable interlude between hymns, or a necessary penance before being allowed to escape into the fresh air.

Even those who write books on preaching collude with the general prejudice. Take some recent titles: *Raising the Dead*; *Surviving the Sermon*; *Pew Rights for Those who have to Listen to Sermons*; *Fresh Air in the Pulpit*; *Short, Sharp and Off the Point*. *Leadership* magazine carries a cartoon showing a preacher asleep in the pulpit. One member of the congregation is saying to his neighbour, 'I think where it all went wrong is when he said, "And everything I'm saying to you, I'm saying to myself"'. More than one writer on preaching has quoted the little boy who said, 'Oh, pay the man, mother, and let us go home'. An article in a national paper begins with the observation that sermons are getting shorter and adds, 'This is a remarkable tribute to the power of intercessory prayer'. And so it goes on and on.

I find all this very odd. On the one hand there is universal agreement that listening to sermons is only slightly less enjoyable than

1

sticking pins in your eyes. On the other hand, the rhetoric of the Church insists that 'the foolishness of preaching' is the ministry of the word, the liturgy proclaims it as feeding the flock, and church architecture raises the pulpit high or gives it a central position.

THE SPEECH IS DEAD; LONG LIVE THE SPEECH

The sermon is under attack. It is seen as moralizing, censorious, 'kinda preachy'. Moreover, it struggles against a televisual and media-saturated culture. The standard inference from this observation is that people are addicted to zapping through television channels; are incapable of concentrating for more than three minutes; expect, as inveterate consumers, to be entertained; are sceptical of authoritative pronouncements and find it impossible to listen to talking heads. The sermon also fares badly in the world of adult education, where interactive methods are prominent. Here it is axiomatic that monologues are very bad ways of teaching anybody anything. And in our darker moments we suspect that this assumption is well-founded, especially when we discover that even our nearest and dearest often cannot recall a word we said by Sunday lunchtime.

Yet, paradoxically, it does not appear that the *speech* is dead. Given that the sermon is universally execrated, there is something strange about the fact that the barrister in court continues to command his fee, the company rep makes his client presentation, the after-dinner speaker has them rolling in the aisles, Channel 5 gives substantial chunks of late-night airtime to stand-up comics and Uncle Arthur is called upon to 'say a few words'. The speech is not dead. So what happened to the sermon?

WHY ARE SERMONS THE 'LOW POINT' IN THE SERVICE?

Since this book is intended to be a workbook, you might like to pause here and suggest your own answers to this question.

On the basis of a lifetime of listening to sermons I offer the following possibilities:

The sermon is the low point when ...

1   I do not really *expect* to hear God speaking, at any rate not through this preacher on this morning. I don't sit with eager anticipation or with a desperate soul-thirst for the living water. If I really thought God was going to address me personally, then I would listen intently and worry at the words like a dog with a bone – or (to change the metaphor) squeeze the fruit until the precious juice oozed out. Too often, as Walter Burghardt puts it, 'You are here because you have to be, because Sunday Mass is a serious obligation, because otherwise there's a chance you may blister in hell'.[1] Or, as William O'Malley advised preachers, assume a complete lack of interest on the part of the congregation: 'Presume they would rather feed their children to crocodiles than listen to you'.[2]

2   The words are *irrelevant*; they do not scratch where I'm itching, or heal my wounds, or speak into my condition. They do not voice for me what I was trying to say but couldn't, because I hadn't got the words. The preacher doesn't sound as if he or she lives in my world, or has any idea of what my life is really like.

3   The preacher isn't speaking a *living* word. It's banal, platitudinous and dull; full of calendar mottoes and generalities. It's predictable and tired. Many, many people have now heard the story of *The Velveteen Rabbit*. They have heard it many times – so many times that they would gladly eat the pie. If I want naive comments on society, politics, the environment, the royal family, computers, the stock exchange, education, I would do better to get my hair cut or take a ride in a taxi. What I hear doesn't reflect the real Gospel, because the real Gospel is always slightly surprising or shocking. What I get is tamed, ordered, buttoned up, prepackaged and monumentally, mind-bendingly dull.

Comments like these point us towards what congregations really want when they settle down to listen to a sermon. It might be useful now to look more closely at the sermon form, to see if we can discover ways of meeting what are, after all, not wholly unreasonable demands. We could begin the enquiry by considering the history of preaching, biblical theology or homiletical theory – but I am more inclined to start with the common-sense understanding of the sermon.

WHAT IS THIS THING CALLED A SERMON?

In my view people have a reasonably clear idea of what a sermon is and what it should sound like. While I was gathering material for this book I asked about 50 ministers in the Durham area if they would let me have a copy of a recent sermon. To their everlasting credit, most of them obliged. I still think it was an act of amazing generosity. From time to time, in the course of this book, I shall use their sermons as illustrative material. (I gave a guarantee that I would only use the texts positively and constructively, so if you come across a sermon which is criticized, it will be one of my own.) Collecting actual sermons in this way has allowed me to define sermons not by reference to Scripture or theology but by analysing what is preached. This is the sermon as it is experienced, enjoyed or endured by congregations in the North East of England.

The standard pattern in most, though not all, sermons ran as follows:

- An *opening*, which appeared to be designed to set the scene, grab the attention and obtain the goodwill of the listeners.
- Some *reference to the Bible*, and an attempt to draw from it a spiritual truth or principle. The Bible was seen as an authoritative book.
- A moment, which we might call *getting personal*, when the Bible message was applied to the lives of the congregation. The clear presumption was that the Bible was relevant, that it was a living word which could shed light on the contemporary situation.
- An *appeal to act* on the message thus distilled and expounded – though the action which congregations were asked to take varied greatly.
- An *assumption*, always implied and sometimes stated, that this speech was in some sense delivered in the name of God, and even as 'a word from God'.

As an example, here is a typical sermon, constructed more or less according to this pattern.

A sermon on gossip

The preacher selected, from the book of Proverbs, five disconnected verses on the theme of gossip.

- The opening referred to the prevalence of gossip, in the world and in the Church, and the fact that it is not taken especially seriously.
- The verses were then expounded in three different ways:

  1 By paraphrase ('In other words ...');

  2 By an interpretation which aimed to expand and deepen the paraphrase ('What it really means is ...');

  3 By making explicit the presumed implications of the verses. These were presented as being wider and broader than the congregation might have imagined: for example, the logic of the verses about gossip was that we should 'speak only those things which are true, kind and necessary'.

- The stakes were then raised by two moves within the sermon which were intended to expose dramatically the real significance of gossip. The first was the use of the term 'fool'. The preacher argued that in the Old Testament, the fool was a person who was in a wrong relationship with God. Therefore gossiping posed the question, 'Are you in a right relationship with God or not?' Both the fool and the gossip were in a wrong relationship: this was what was really at stake. The second move was an appeal to apply these texts personally and ask, 'Lord, is it I? Is it I?' This specific allusion to the Last Supper and Judas' betrayal framed gossiping as very serious indeed. It was almost set on a level with betraying Christ.
- An explicit appeal to action was made. An implicit appeal had already been made in the reference to speaking only 'true, kind and necessary' words. The formal appeal consisted of the injunction, 'And God says, "Don't gossip!"'

- Implicit in the whole sermon was the assumption that this was a message from God to the congregation.

THE CHARACTERISTICS OF PREACHING

This analysis illustrates some of the distinctive features of preaching.

1 It is *authoritative* speech. To begin a sermon with a statement, 'In the name of God ...', or a prayer, 'May I speak in the name of God ...', is to raise the stakes somewhat higher than, 'I'd now like to say a few words'. The preacher stands in a long tradition which goes back at least as far as the 'Hear the word of the Lord' of the Old Testament prophets.

God help me?

2 It is *personally revealing* speech. In Phillips Brooks' words, 'Preaching is truth embodied in personality'. The character and theology of the preacher are all too obvious. It is very difficult for preachers to hide behind the text. The minute they move away from quotation into paraphrase, extending the paraphrase, drawing out the implication and driving home the message, they have to put their heads above the parapet.

3 It is *crafted* speech. The sermon is a carefully devised 15 minutes of rhetoric. To say this is not to insist that any one sermon form is the right one; a successful sermon can take any number of forms. Nevertheless, sermons usually don't just happen: they are plotted.

4 It is *persuasive* speech. The purpose of preaching is to change things, or, to be more precise, to change people. Preaching tries to *do* something, to make a difference. It is not too high-flown to say that it aims at transformation.

> Each of these marks of the sermon – authoritative speech, personally revealing speech, crafted speech, persuasive speech – raises important issues and difficult questions. Each one is both a source of encouragement and a dreadful warning. Jot down your own thoughts on the particular encouragements and dangers of each.

My own reflections run along these lines.

Authoritative speech

A SOURCE OF ENCOURAGEMENT
As a preacher you do not speak on your own authority. This is a very encouraging thought. These are not 'a few thoughts of my own' jotted down on the back of an envelope. When preaching, you bear witness to God; you pass on a word which you have heard in the silence; you rest on the fact that you have been summoned, which is why you can speak, like Jesus, 'with authority'.

A DREADFUL WARNING
The danger is that, after a while, you can get a taste for this sort of thing and start to assume that your words have descended from Sinai. Crenshaw wrote a book called, *Trembling at the Threshold of a Biblical Text*. Quite so. Take your shoes off and cover your face.

Personally revealing speech

A SOURCE OF ENCOURAGEMENT
Amazingly, God has things to say that he can say only through you, through your particular personality, in your accent and in your words. It is just typical of God to incarnate his word, so that just for a moment a human being can enjoy the inestimable privilege of becoming, in George Herbert's phrase, 'a window' for God's grace.

A DREADFUL WARNING
There are few better opportunities for an ego trip than the sermon, and the pulpit can license the most excruciatingly self-indulgent revelations. Blissfully unaware of the effect he's having on the embarrassed congregation, the preacher continues to spill out his entrails on the altar of self-disclosure. The listeners squirm and pray that they might disappear down a crack between the flagstones. And his teenage children contemplate parricide.

Crafted speech

A SOURCE OF ENCOURAGEMENT

Time spent crafting the sermon is not wasted and does not represent a failure to trust the Holy Spirit. I like the story of the preacher who met an enthusiastic friend. 'You don't mean to tell me you've been spending time preparing a sermon, do you?', said the friend. 'Next time you preach, don't prepare, just go up into the pulpit and the Holy Spirit will speak to you.' 'Really?', said the preacher, 'All right, I'll try it.' The following week he met the man again. 'Well, did you try it? 'Yes.' 'And did the Holy Spirit speak to you?' 'Yes, he did.' 'What did he say?' 'He said, "You have been very lazy."'

A DREADFUL WARNING

The danger of crafting the speech is that you can come to rely upon your cunning techniques. Manipulating the congregation isn't faithful preaching. A sermon which relies on shouting loudly or 'a touching, affecting story' qualifies for the Sounding Brass and Tinkling Cymbal award.

Persuasive speech

A SOURCE OF ENCOURAGEMENT

People really are *changed* as a result of preaching. Some preaching, some of the time, does have dramatic results. If you can remember sermons when God spoke to you then the chances are that members of your congregation will. Of course, much preaching resembles regular breakfasts – essential but unmemorable. Nevertheless, the knowledge that God does speak to people through your words ought to lead to considerable excitement. W. E. Sangster said that as preachers climbed the pulpit steps they should be saying, 'Let me get at 'em!'

A DREADFUL WARNING

The down-side of this feature of preaching is that you can get discouraged when your best efforts at persuasion do not produce instant transformations every week. Preaching is much criticized for having little effect. After months with no visible results, there is a natural temptation to lose heart, especially when there seems to be more response from the bodies under the flagstones than those in the pews.

GOING FORWARD

These four characteristics suggest a way forward for those of us who want to go on preaching even in a chilly world. They invite us to look seriously at our foundation text and the way in which we listen to God through it. They also suggest that we ought to work at knowing ourselves a little better, unashamedly allowing God to refract his word through our personalities without making that an excuse to blow our own trumpets. Again, it will not be time wasted if we study our craft, working on techniques, skills and that dirty word, rhetoric. Finally, we also need to clarify what we are trying to do, not letting ourselves be overwhelmed by the magnitude of the word 'transformation', and setting ourselves to know our hearers more clearly and love them more dearly.

Here, at the point at which we start to gird our loins for the journey ahead, I offer an encouraging thought from John Calvin: '*Voilà* the pulpit, which is the throne of God.'

PART ONE

Hearing the Word

1 The passage, the whole passage and nothing but the passage

I may as well get my prejudices out of the way at the start. In this book I want to argue in favour of Bible-based preaching. I have already tried to indicate that, whatever one's personal understanding of biblical inspiration and authority may be, the Bible contains the primary documents of the faith. The Church is formed by Scripture. Scripture ought to be at the heart of every piece of distinctively Christian communication.

> You might like to stop here and react to this paragraph. Can you foresee defects in this (over)confident prescription? What place does the Bible hold in your preaching? Do you warm to, or groan at, the phrase, 'expository preaching'? Have you already pigeonholed me as a naive fundamentalist?

I realize that not all sermons are focused explicitly on the Bible, and in practice they come in all shapes and sizes. Some consist of comment on a contemporary issue; others take the form of a presentation of what Christians believe about a topic or theme; yet others will be designed as a meditation on an aspect of human experience, or the explanation of a doctrine, or the defence of Christian faith against some objection or difficulty. The Bible does not have to be quoted extensively or referred to in every sermon.

Christian communication can be biblical without mentioning the Bible. Nevertheless, it ought to be possible to relate all sermons back to the biblical witness, and, for my money, most sermons ought to concentrate on a Bible passage.

I do not believe that this focus constitutes a straitjacket. In fact, when I studied the 'Durham sermons', I noticed that most gave the Bible a central place, even though the theological positions of the preachers varied considerably. Moreover, where a sermon was not drawn from a Bible text or passage, it still drew on the Bible for its key ideas. It might have been in a passing allusion to the incarnation, or in a comment which assumed the reality of judgement, or in an exhortation to see Christ in others – but whatever the reference, the sermons were controlled by, and echoed, biblical truths.

A few examples will illustrate how this worked in practice. In the sermons I collected there was a general assumption, whether explicitly stated or implicit, that the Bible:

- would provide parallels with the congregation's situation: 'Nehemiah refused to use power for his own gain'; 'If Habukkuk complained then so may we';
- could be used to prevent fruitless speculation: 'We search the Scriptures to test our opinions';
- contained authoritative truth: 'The *parousia* is not really about clouds and angels – it is really about presence' (said after the preacher had drawn a distinction between outward trimmings and inner meaning);
- was a source of spiritual principles: 'If God chooses to become human, then he affirms our humanity and makes us special'; 'Every healing is a sign of the healing which awaits us all';
- offered a privileged perspective: 'Here is a story of which the end is known. From the vantage point it affords, we can speak confidently about our own story. This is what is really going on'.

It is clear that, for these preachers, the Bible was seen as a special book. Referring to its message was not on a level with quoting Shakespeare or the *Daily Mirror*. Most spoke as if this book was the appointed place of God's conversation with us, and the clearest window into Christ; it was the master tape.

EXPOUNDING THE WORD

In keeping with these assumptions, I want to recommend that most preaching ought to consist of the exposition of a biblical text. This proposal needs some explanation, however.

First, the word 'exposition' is ambiguous. It is often used in a restricted sense and taken to mean a verse-by-verse analytical commentary on the text. I make no such assumption. By exposition I mean *any* process which will ensure that the essential meaning and force of the text is communicated. The means by which this is done will vary considerably. Indeed, faithful exposition may not always be recognizable as a sermon – a point I wish to develop in a later section. Nevertheless a biblical text will lie at the bottom of any truly Christian communication.

A second issue concerns what constitutes a text. An older type of preaching always began the sermon with a 'text' in the sense of a verse (or even a part of a verse). This convention is still not unknown. The problem with this is that the text (in this abbreviated sense) can be no more than a nod in the direction of the Bible. Once the cap has been doffed, the preacher is free to pursue his or her own route without the need for further acknowledgement. Even in those cases where the text is the framework of the sermon, there is no overriding need to set that single verse in a larger context. Congregations exposed to this style of preaching are seldom encouraged to get a grasp of the sweep of the story, the argument of the letter or the movement of the psalmist's meditation. Texts easily become pretexts – pegs on which the preacher can hang thoughts which may or may not illuminate the Bible passage. This is one reason why my own preference is for a passage long enough to do justice to the original author's intention, in as far as this is ascertainable.

It is thus my hope that preaching will normally consist of the exposition of a passage. I want to press this point, because it is the assumption on which this book is based. If this principle is accepted, then the Bible passage becomes the focus of all our attention. When we do concentrate on the individual passage, however, we are confronted with some interesting issues.

THE FORM OF THE REVELATION

I begin by asking, not entirely flippantly, 'If the Bible is God's revelation of himself and his purposes to humankind, then why has he given it to us in such an inefficient way?' As a handbook on life and how to live it, it is surpassed in incoherence only by computer manuals. The contents page contains such snappy titles as 'Obadiah' and '2 Peter'. We can hardly wait to dip into this! Surely it would have made for greater clarity if God had organized what he wanted to say in a logical order with intelligible headings. Perhaps something like a handbook of systematic theology would have made everything that much more lucid. A better job all round.

Instead of telling God how to run the universe, perhaps it would be more useful to take the question really seriously. Why has the biblical revelation come down to us in such an untidy form? This question can be answered at the human level, in which case the explanation will trace a lengthy process of oral tradition, selection, redaction and conservation. But if you enquire of God, then you don't so much get an answer as end up with a different question. Frankly, we have no idea why God has chosen this way of communicating. He just has. The question we're left with is, 'What are we going to do about it?' For whatever reason, God has given us the revelation in a form which is messy, often communicated through stories but also through letters, complaints, laws, taunt songs and sermons – and always filtered through personalities who reflect and speak out of highly specific situations. The Bible has a unity and a common theme, but it also exhibits considerable diversity. Sometimes one part of the book has to be considered in tension with another. A dramatic example is the tension between Proverbs and Ecclesiastes. One says, 'This is the way to live. Try it and you find that we are right'. The other says, 'We did try it. And it isn't. And you're not.' This untidy, piecemeal, highly diverse collection of writings looks like an invitation to follow the twists and turns of a story, or join in a continuing dialogue. This is the Bible as we have it. We might feel, modestly, that we could have done better than God but, in the event, he didn't ask us to take on this particular project. We shouldn't be surprised. The embodiment, or the incarnation, of truth in specific people and situations seems to be his preferred style of working.

To return to the question above: 'Given that this is the Bible as I receive it, what am I going to do about it?' Or, to put the issue another way, 'If I take *the form* of the revelation seriously, what might be its implications for me as a preacher?'

THE UNIQUENESS OF A PASSAGE

One very important implication might be that any particular passage in front of me has to be taken very seriously indeed. Spelled out, that means that each passage has something distinctive to say – or at least, I ought to approach it with that assumption. Let me raise the stakes a little: *God has something to say through this particular passage which he has chosen not to say in any other way.* As preachers, standing barefoot on holy ground, we had better not assume that we can dilute a passage, or distil its message, without loss, or substitute some other text for it, or assume that it is saying pretty much the same as some other passage. If we do, we shall miss the distinctiveness, the authentic accents of this word just as surely as if we assumed that all Australians were more or less like Edna Everage. This passage is unique.

We can see the effect of ignoring this statement when we approach the stories of the nativity and the passion. It is quite difficult to hear what Matthew and Luke want to tell us about the birth of Jesus because 2,000 years of Christian devotion have stitched together their accounts. Innumerable nativity plays have ground into our consciousness a continuing story which begins with Zechariah and Elisabeth, neatly inserts Gabriel's message to Joseph, gets Mary and Joseph to Bethlehem to the stable, calls up shepherds and wise men (in that order) and takes the holy family to Egypt at the end. But what is lost in this process is any sense of Matthew's distinctive presentation of Christ. He cannot speak to us because we keep insisting that Luke must butt in – and vice versa. Reading either Matthew or Luke as if you had never heard of the other evangelist is an exciting and liberating experience.

Much the same happens with the passion narratives. Mark presents us with a Jesus who is utterly abandoned. He hangs on the cross deserted by everyone: his cry of dereliction even accuses God; those crucified with him abuse him; the passers-by taunt him. But many three-hour Good Friday services have led us to hear that story only as part of a larger synthesis which includes the penitent thief, the cry of triumph, 'Father, forgive', and 'Into thy hands I commend my spirit'. If you read Mark as if you had never looked at the other gospels, then Mark's particular emphases can be heard clear and sharp.

> The exercise of reading a passion narrative as if the other gospels did not exist can be an exhilarating (and moving) experience. Can I recommend that you try it with one of the other three gospels?[1]

EVEN THE AWKWARD BITS ...

If a passage has something special to say then I ought to listen to it – and this implies listening to all of it. Most of us are familiar with looking at a Bible reading in order to grab the first preachable 'lesson' that pops up. The text offers us a pretext. It gives us an excuse to preach on a topic or theme dear to our hearts which is, by an extraordinary stroke of luck, mentioned in the passage. This is the Bible-passage-as-peg-to-hang-thoughts-on school of preaching. Even the famous preachers can do it. The pulpit giant, Harry Emerson Fosdick, had a standard sermon on 'The three dimensions of a whole life'. He based this firmly (?) on an exposition of the vision of the new Jerusalem in the book of Revelation, in which the celestial city happened to be 100 cubits in each dimension. On this convenient peg he was able to hang his own particular combination of psycho-social-spiritual exhortation.

Trying to do justice to the whole passage is often very difficult, because we find it easier to leave out those verses which don't fit. I once asked a group what they thought might come out of Mark's account of the healing of the leper (Mark 1.40–45). One person thought she might preach on Jesus' healing ministry. Another decided that the sermon should deal with 'ways in which we spoil God's plans', on the grounds that the leper's announcement of his healing forced Jesus to revise his strategy. I suppose it's just possible that these are the points which Mark intends to make, but the suggestions left me uneasy.

> You might like to pause at this point and ask yourself how you read Mark 1.40–45. To what extent do you agree with the suggestions made? Do they leave out any features of the story?

My unease arose from the feeling that both embryonic sermons seemed not to do justice to particular emphases of the passage, and looked as though they intended to gloss over or ignore the surprising or awkward bits of the story. For example, don't we need to do *something* with a Jesus 'filled with anger' (the better reading of verse 41, rather than 'moved with pity')? And we are confronted with a Jesus who snorts. Our translations soften the original with something like 'sternly charged', but the commentaries draw our attention to a noise (of anger, exasperation?), which needs explanation. Then Jesus 'drives the man out' – a verb usually associated with the exorcism of demons not the after-care of healed lepers. Somewhere we ought to try to include comment on Jesus' command to go to the priest 'as a testimony *against* them', or 'a proof that you are cured' (but which? It makes a difference). And Jesus *touched* him! The phrase would surely have been significant to the first readers. What will we make of it? Here are surprises enough to be getting on with, but the passage is not properly 'heard' until they have been wrestled with and some sense made of them. I leave you to work on the story with the help of the commentaries.

The temptation not to notice the awkward bits afflicts us all. A set lesson might be helpfully cut just before the difficult point. For instance, a reading from Isaiah 6 will often concentrate on the prophet's vision in the temple, but conclude at the ringing response, '"Here am I. Send me!"' Alas, the original passage continues for another five verses. True, these are some of the most difficult verses of the book – but they are also the verses on which the New Testament chooses to focus. I remember a friend of mine preaching a fine sermon on John 1.1–14 ('the Word was made flesh') but, understandably, leaving out all reference to John the Baptist, 'the man sent from God' in verses 6–8. I realize that these verses interrupt a purple passage, almost a poem, on the Word – but the author of the Fourth Gospel obviously thought that they were important enough to set them in a prominent position. Don't we need to take them into account?

My main point here is that if we ignore parts of the passage, or use it as a pretext for some message of our own, we devalue the word which we have been given. It is not allowed to speak in its own distinctive tone. The Bible becomes, in Craddock's phrase, 'wallpaper or background music'. However tricky the passage, we are called to wrestle with it, even if it speaks in an alien tongue and sets us intractable problems of interpretation.

KANGAROOS AND HOBBY HORSES

The logic of the position I'm proposing is that we shall try to stay within the specific passage in front of us, and not dot around the rest of the Bible as if we were so many kangaroos. Marsupial preaching can be very tiring for congregations, who are required to hop after the preacher as he or she bounds through Leviticus, 1 Kings and Jude in swift succession. The congregation realizes that the preacher has been at the concordance again, and longs for a less omnivorous appetite.

More seriously, preaching in this all-inclusive, systematizing manner often results in flattening the message of the Bible. I once read a commentary on Jeremiah, and at the end I suddenly realized that I had been told a great deal more about Paul's epistle to the Romans than Jeremiah. But if Jeremiah's message is constantly assimilated into Pauline theology, the prophet is never allowed to speak for himself. Similarly, not every psalm of complaint needs to be resolved into comforting conclusions: give it space and time to say what it wants to say. Not every passage in the Bible contains the 'whole counsel of God'. There was once a Scottish Baptist minister who preached on the prodigal son. It was a classic three-point sermon on the themes of rejection, repentance and restoration. Having come to the end, he leaned over the edge of the pulpit and said, 'And now a wee word about baptism'. Alas, there isn't anything about baptism in the story of the prodigal son.

Such moves do not necessarily make for bad sermons. George Whitefield preached a storming sermon on the burning bush. In a blistering sequence he made the following points:

> The burning bush is a type of the Church because it is 'a little bush of briars and thorns', 'not a tall cedar'; while it is in the world it burns with fiery trials but these are God's purifying fire; God spoke out of the bush and this is a sign that 'my people shall burn to the end of time but I will succour them – when they burn I will burn too'; to our shame Christ can dwell in the bush when we Christians find it impossible to live together under one roof; 'our suffering times will be our best times'; though the bush is burning let it not be consumed but burn 'higher and higher' until it 'shall be translated to the paradise of God', where there will be no burning bush except the fire of love; the sinner is the burning bush, burning with foppery, nonsense and pride and unless he repents he will burn in Hell and not be consumed; 'O firebrands of Hell, may God pluck you as a brand out of that burning'; 'O God, turn the burning bushes of the Devil into the burning bushes of the Son of God'.

A robust sermon. It is also profoundly biblical, in that almost everything Whitefield says is to be found in Scripture – yet the reader is left with the nagging thought: 'Yes, all very powerful stuff but has any of it anything to do with the story in Exodus 3?'

I underline the requirement to preach on the passage, the whole passage and nothing but the passage out of a respect for Scripture and the God who speaks through it. The sermon that is based on the passage is controlled by the passage. I do not have a licence to say everything I feel like saying (but only what is in the passage); what I say is shaped by what the passage says and the way in which it says it; the passage will have a life of its own; will not be domesticated or sanitized by my selecting only material which I find 'suitable' and 'relevant'. This strategy will deliver me from saying the same thing every time or riding my hobby horses. I believe also that it implies that God has things to say which I may not have thought of, and that the Bible can, like God, stand over against me, to disconcert, surprise, challenge and disturb.

2 Beyond the sacred page

This chapter will suggest a checklist of methods for engaging with a Bible passage in an attempt to hear afresh what it has to say. It is no more than one possible checklist among dozens. It's a cluster of things to try, not the combination to a safe: you cannot work systematically through the code and watch the deposit box of holy truth spring open at your say-so. If God speaks through the Bible, then we had better concentrate on the fact that he is sovereign. He does what he wants, and does not come to heel when we snap our fingers.

Nevertheless there is still some merit in trying different ways of hearing afresh what the text says, and of attempting to become the 'attentive reader', sensitive to every nuance. The text is an ancient one and that brings its own problems. We cannot be absolutely sure what it meant to those who heard it first. Despite this, faithful preaching begins with faithful reading. We approach the Bible as a kind of ideal reader, and take it with full imaginative seriousness. To help us do this we can make use of at least at eight different strategies.

1 RESPECTING THE LITERARY FORM

Many preachers treat the biblical passage as if it were the ingredients of a cake, lying on the working surface, collected more or less at random. The ingredients don't really possess any shape: they are dutifully waiting for the cook to mix, knead, season, pop into the oven and produce in an edible form 40 minutes later. But this analogy suggests that the ingredients have merely been assembled and that the real work begins with the preacher. The facts of the matter are that the biblical passage has already been shaped. A preacher who ignores the literary form of the passage is like a cook who takes taking an already existing cake and breaks it up in order to use the crumbs as ingredients for a totally different dish.

I emphasize this point because form creates expectations. Take the limerick, for example. The opening line is almost certainly going to set up a particular kind of mind-set. 'There was a young lady of Hythe ...' – there can't be many people who expect a serious, solemn or moving communication to follow. I once challenged a group of students to produce a serious limerick on a religious theme. I don't think it can be done. Two of the efforts I received were as follows:

> From God and his Spirit I flew
> And thought all things Christian taboo.
> Someone took me to church,
> where God gave me the urge
> To know Jesus, who made me anew.

> For God, he so loved all the earth
> That he showed us how much we were worth,
> By sending his son
> To bring salvation,
> And to give us the chance of new birth.

I rest my case!

What is happening is that the form of the poem is so strong that we cannot hear the content in any other way than as dumpty-dum doggerel – which rather detracts from the seriousness of the thought.

A psalm of lament or complaint – and there seem to be rather a lot of them in the Psalter – invites us by its *form* to enter its dark and angry mood, and respond to it in those terms. As form critics work on the psalms, they help us to see how the particular grammar of Psalm 22, for example, raises the stakes. 'My God, my God, why have you forsaken me?' goes considerably further than the usual complaint form. We would expect something like, 'I said to my soul, why has the Lord forsaken me?' – but this softens the complaint by making it a third-person address to the soul. 'Do not hide yourself from me, O Lord' (v. 19) turns it into a prayer. What we have in Psalm 22, however, is a direct, naked accusation. 'You have abandoned me! Why?' The passage will not yield its disturbing treasures to those who want to ignore this feature, soften the complaints and hurry on to a comforting and 'positive' conclusion.

Form is significant. A letter may be a closely reasoned argument, it may be a set of *ad hoc* responses, more or less on the hoof, dashed off to sort out a congregation in crisis or confusion. A taunt song is a piece of satire; it is not a hymn of praise. A list of proverbs asks to be read in a different way from a kaleidoscope of apocalyptic visions. It may not always be possible to preach in a way which reflects the form of the passage but we ought always to have the form of the passage in the forefront of our minds when we are trying to read it responsibly.

2 ATTENDING TO THE CONTEXT

It is a dangerous exercise to interpret words out of context. Once, when reversing my car into a narrow gap, I asked my wife, 'What am I like at the back?' Her response was neither task-related nor guaranteed to boost my self-esteem. Context helps us fill in the unspoken gaps between the words, and hear the silent comments which festoon themselves around the page. Context means looking closely at the setting and occasion of the passage. The likely historical context of the cry, 'Comfort, comfort my people' (Isaiah 40), is the end of a long and bitter exile in a strange land. This setting does not invite us to read the passage as an assertion that there is no redemption without repentance and forgiveness. We shall be closer to the heart of the prophet's message if we read it as a song of hope, a proclamation of good news worth shouting from the mountain top. After all, the prophet is even inclined to say that the people have been hammered enough – they 'have received double for all their sins'. 'Give them a break, Lord.' And he is going to! Trying to reconstruct the likely historical context is always worthwhile. For example, if Ruth and Jonah were written as literature of protest against a harsh policy of ethnic cleansing, then we have an important clue about the way in which they should be read. 'The only good Gentile is a dead Gentile', says the establishment. The book of Jonah says, 'Look how these Gentiles pray in a crisis when the so-called prophet of Israel is fast asleep. And look how they repent when they hear the word of God. Meanwhile the prophet sulks under a tree.'

Nevertheless, we should not despair if the historical setting is beyond us. In the case of Jonah and Ruth, we probably have all we need within the stories themselves. The content of these books sets up tensions with other parts of the Old Testament, whether our hypothetical historical reconstruction is correct or not. There is a literary context which involves us in looking at the wider setting of the passage: it asks us to examine the whole drift of the book – the plot of the gospel or the argument of the letter. Does the cleansing of the temple in John shed light on the miracle of turning water into wine at Cana? They both come in chapter 2 and bounce off one other. In Luke 18, Jesus heals a blind man just after the writer has told us that the disciples 'did not know what Jesus was talking about'. Context is another way of pointing up the fact that a specific passage is likely to be part of a larger, crafted, shaped, designed piece. This is another reason why it may be unhelpful to preach from an individual text: it is too easy to detach it from its moorings and float off into the ocean of our own pet thoughts.

3   TRACING THE PLOT

Narrative is narrative; it is not systematic theology. In stories, events occur in an order decided by the author. He may not give them to us in the order in which they occurred – and he may have his own reasons for keeping us in the dark. We grasp the message and force of a narrative when we read it carefully from beginning to end as if we were reading it for the first time. How many sermons on Abraham's call to sacrifice Isaac suffer because they work on the assumption that the end is known from the beginning? The Bible keeps the denouement – the ram caught in a thicket – till the end.

As far as Old Testament narratives are concerned, it may help to bear in mind some of the rules about understanding them. On a great many occasions the essential message is carried by a *speech* delivered at a critical point in the story. For example, in the story of the fiery furnace (Daniel 3), the heroes, Shadrach, Meshach and Abednego, are allowed by the narrator to speak only once – but their words encapsulate the point of the story: 'Your Majesty, we will not try to defend ourselves. If the God whom we serve is able to save us from the blazing furnace and from your power, then he will. *But even if he doesn't,* your Majesty may be sure that we will not worship your god, and we will not bow down to the gold statue that you have set up' (Good News Bible). Again, it is worth taking account of *repetitions* in a story; they may well point up key ideas. And the narrator always sits in the seat of authority and from a godlike vantage point tells you what is really going on. 'Some time later God tested Abraham'; 'But the Lord was not pleased with what David had done' (GNB).

> The story of David and Goliath in 1 Samuel 17 satisfyingly illustrates these principles. Try to identify key speeches, repetitions and authoritative narration.

You probably picked up the following motifs:

- Israel's enemies defy Israel and the living God;
- Israel responds with fear;
- David is disdained by everybody;
- David is confident that God will deliver him;
- God does not deliver with the sword.

Reading in the light of the principles set out above cues us in to what the story is trying to say.

4 ASKING WHAT THE TEXT IS TRYING TO DO

Biblical texts do things to people. It is easy to read them as if they just made a series of statements about God, life, the universe and everything. They do not just contain information, however: they are also designed to move, persuade, convince, comfort, transform, inspire and convict us. The Bible is designed to make something happen to us. No one is intended to go away saying, 'Well, there's a thing! How very interesting.' The characteristic response to the message of the Bible is that of the pilgrims on the day of Pentecost:

'What shall we do?' – or Job's, 'I am ashamed of all I have said and repent in dust and ashes' (GNB).

An important factor in hearing a text clearly is letting it say what it wants to say, and do what it wants to do. Texts do inform us – but the imparting of new information is probably not their main purpose: we also need to let their force or impact strike us. In the same way, the words 'I love you' are rather more than the communication of information: they are intended to have an effect and transform a situation. Revelation involves seeing something in sharp focus and encountering a whole new world. No one can see the world differently, particularly where God and self are involved, without his or her emotions being profoundly stirred. Readings of the Bible which ignore this feature result in preaching which is cool, correct and distant.

I wonder whether the question, 'What is the text trying to do?', isn't the most important one to ask. So many Bible studies begin with some sort of Noddy-type question like, 'Look at verses 1–4. What 13 things are said about God in these verses?' Answers come out like, 'God is holy, compassionate, active ...' But the passage under scrutiny may be using those attributes of God to fuel a blistering complaint about God's lack of interest in the writer, or to call all Israel to praise, or ensure that the readers are lost in wonder and adoration, or to assert God's greatness in contrast to humanity's folly or to chide the hardhearted, or to rehearse ancient and traditional truths in order to persuade Israel that God may be trusted in some risky enterprise. On its own, 'God is great' tells me little. What is the writer trying to *do*?

Look at Luke 4.1–13, the temptation of Jesus. What do you think Luke was trying to *do* to his readers by presenting the story in this way? Is he trying to foster an attitude, correct an error, provoke a disclosure, encourage the dispirited, celebrate a truth? Or what?

Your response will depend partly on what you think Luke is trying to achieve in writing the double volume Luke–Acts. That will be matter of trying to pick up his main themes and emphases and to relate the temptation story to them.

Here are some possibilities.

Luke hoped:

- To shape the Church's mission strategy. The Church in its mission must avoid taking easy ways – choosing the good over the best, compromising with the world, putting its trust in sensationalism.
- To encourage Christians in temptation. Christians should not be discouraged when they are tempted since Jesus himself had to undergo temptation.
- To forewarn Christians about times of trial. Christians should not be surprised by times of trial, since Christ's temptations followed immediately after a profound spiritual experience at the Jordan.
- To redefine the Christian identity. Christians who follow Christ are part of the new Israel, since Christ's replies to the tempter present him as the fulfilment of Israel's vocation.

5 EXPOSING THE STRUCTURE

The particular emphases of a passage may best be exposed by trying to uncover its underlying framework or skeleton. Modern commentaries often set these out very helpfully – however, there is nothing to match attempting to do the exercise for oneself. Unfortunately most translations disturb the original structure in the process of turning an ancient language into English. Comparing translations may help, but here is one argument for trying to learn at least enough Greek to spot a main verb with its connected participles. Like a teacher with her class on a day-trip to the zoo, the Greek sentence trots along with the main verb in charge and the participial phrases kept firmly subordinate. But the analysis gives you a clue about the relative importance of the different verbs.

A second source of help lies in signpost words, like 'accordingly', 'but', 'in order that', 'therefore', which point the way to the logic of the following sentence or paragraph. Older preachers used to say, 'Whenever you see a "Therefore" ask yourself, "Wherefore the therefore?"' It's good advice.

> Read Colossians 1.28–9 in a number of different trans-
> lations or, if possible, in the original. Set out its structure in
> diagrammatic form.

For what it's worth, here is my effort (based on my own literal trans-
lation of the Greek).

Whom (i.e. 'Christ', first word in the sentence, probably
emphatic) *we proclaim* (main verb – in charge)
> *warning everyone*
> *and teaching every one* (there are two elements in proclaim-
ing)
> > *in all wisdom*
In order that (signpost word – 'why are we doing this?') *we may
present every one* (the third 'every' and the same word as the
'all' in 'all wisdom')
> > *perfect / mature in Christ.*

To this end (signpost word) *I also labour / toil* (strong word)
> *struggling* (another strong word – this is a battle and it
> looks as if it is all up to Paul)
> > *according to his energy / strength*
> > > *energizing in me in power* (aha, I see – everything
> > > depends on Paul and everything depends on God).

6 WORKING AT BINARY OPPOSITIONS

We often point up the meaning of a text by using contrasts. We set
dark against light, inside against outside, life against death, and so
on. These oppositions can sometimes act as clues to the underlying
organization of the passage.

Read Colossians 2.6–19. Here Paul structures his argument by means of an almost bewildering display of contrasts. Try to set these out in two columns in order to bring to the surface Paul's assumptions about the Christian faith.

You might have noted the following:

teachings handed down by men	the wisdom of Christ
slavery	freedom
empty deceit	fullness in Christ
the shadow of things in the future	the reality or substance is Christ
ruling spirits of the universe	he led them as captives in his victory procession
circumcision made by men	circumcision made by Christ
buried	raised
spiritually dead	brought to life
the head of the body	the joints and ligaments

The effect of all these opposing ideas is to drive the reader towards the conclusion, 'Jesus Christ is the real thing!' Christ is linked with what is divine, real, life-giving, triumphant, free. Death and deception are at work in the world around us. We begin to discern the controlling impulses in Paul's argument.

7   SYSTEMATICALLY USING THE SENSES

We can come to a deeper understanding by working through the passage, with each of our five senses, living in the story, using our imagination but allowing it to be disciplined by the text. This is not the place for wild flights of fancy. You know what I mean:

Imagine, if you will, the home life of our Lord and see him now playing with the wood shavings under Joseph's workbench. I am quite sure he was happy to be there. And when he became a man and had his own business, I am sure that any yoke he made would have been a sturdy one but with the rough edges lovingly and skilfully smoothed away ...

Rather than turn into biblical Catherine Cooksons, we work through the passage, taking it with full imaginative seriousness. Ask yourself the questions, 'What am I hearing here? Or seeing? Or smelling? Touching? Tasting?'

> Read Isaiah 6.1–13. Now work through the story with each of your five senses, living in the story, using your imagination but allowing it to be disciplined by the text.

On one occasion, when a group tried this method of unlocking the text, two fascinating points emerged in discussion. The first was that few members of the group had appreciated that the prophet was involved in something akin to a earthquake ('the posts of the door moved at the voice of them who cried') – an experience which makes sense of the cry, '"Woe is me! I am lost!"' (NRSV). The second insight gained by this method was summed up in the reaction of one reader: 'I can smell burning flesh'. Here, truths about forgiveness and cleansing are embodied in the image of cauterizing (a burning coal, taken from the altar with the tongs, and laid upon the prophet's mouth). Any sermon which comes out of this reading will therefore need to take account of the mood of the passage. In fact, this exercise makes you wonder if the writer of the hymn, 'Bright the vision that delighted once the sight of Judah's seer', had ever read Isaiah 6. *Delighted?* Surely not.

What happens at the next stage – the sermon-writing stage? Well, one sermon which tried to be faithful to the passage ended up with three headings as follows:

• an encounter with God in terms of terror;
• an experience of forgiveness in terms of pain;
• an understanding of ministry in terms of burden.

You can see how the direction and mood of the sermon has been controlled by reading the text 'through the senses'.

8   FINDING THE SURPRISE

In his influential book *Preaching*, Fred Craddock writes about 'looking for trouble'; looking for the surprise is a similar idea. If you read a passage carefully, imaginatively and prayerfully, the text will often 'pop' – that is, some aspect of the passage will surprise you or scandalize you or puzzle you. This is the feature which it is most tempting to overlook, and this is the bump in the terrain which will tell you where to dig for buried treasure. We have already seen one source of surprise or trouble in Mark 1.40–45, the cleansing of the leper. However, 'surprise' does not primarily refer to difficulties and knotty problems. Surprises are precisely those elements which jolt us out of our complacency, which are beyond expectation and which thrust God's way of seeing things up against our taken-for-granted world. It might be a phrase in a parable of the one who is lost, 'until he find it'; it might be an extraordinary picture of the risen Christ eating a bit of broiled fish, or 'making as if to move on' when the disciples reached Emmaus; it might be a delicate touch of the narrator's art (in the story of Hagar, only God has the decency to call the slave woman by her name). You just have to believe that the passage will 'pop' if you give it time.

THE NECESSARY STRUGGLE

Here are some of the strategies we might use in order to engage with a passage faithfully, imaginatively and responsibly. It is *necessary* work, since the way in which we read the passage directly affects the word which we have to bring to the congregation, and without this discipline we are likely to make do with a few choice thoughts of our own. It is also *hard* work, and we might wonder how much of all this effort needs to appear in the sermon. We don't like to waste research, particularly research into the original languages or the world of the text. My impression is that most congregations are pretty happy to let us get on with it, once they feel they can trust us. So for my money, we ought not skimp on the study, but we don't have to parade our learning.

PART TWO

Discerning a Message

3 What's cooking?

How can we move from the biblical passage to a preachable message? There is a naive view which supposes that the message can be 'read off' from the text – that the moral, the message or the meaning exists in the text independently of our reading of it. All we have to do is to think hard, pray hard, read carefully – and the preachable message will pop out, like toast from a toaster, into our hands.

We might think that we would be pretty safe with a close para-phrase, for example. We go through the passage verse by verse, or small section by small section, and through never straying far from the text we ensure that the message of the passage is safely injected into the listeners without fear of contamination. But even the closest paraphrase, once it becomes a paraphrase, involves a trans-lation. And as soon as the exercise stops being just a restatement of 'what this might have meant to the original author or readers' (not that *that* is always a particularly easy thing to state confidently), our paraphrase entails a series of personal decisions about the contem-porary meaning and relevance of the passage.

Some of the time-honoured methods of moving from text to sermon should warn us that it may not be as simple as we suppose. Powerful sermons have been preached on the Good Samaritan which trace the journey of humankind from the heavenly city to death, via being attacked by Satan, left half-dead by the Law, rescued by Christ, and received by the Church. In the process, the true meaning of the oil and wine, and of the two pence, can be revealed to the admiring but slightly surprised congregations. But at the end we wonder if that is really the message which should come out of the parable.

Spurgeon cited a similar piece of pulpit ingenuity in a sermon on the nighthawk, the owl and the cuckoo, which are all unclean birds under the Levitical law. According to the preacher, nighthawks are people who pilfer on the sly, or adulterate their goods and cheat their neighbours without being suspected of being rogues. Owls are drunkards because they are liveliest at night, or 'professors of religion' as they are small birds which look big because they puff out their feathers. Cuckoos are clergy who utter the same note whenever they open their mouths in church and live off other birds' eggs! Spurgeon's reaction was: 'My carnal eyes cannot see it in the text'.[1]

These methods look suspect because we sense that they cannot be connected to the biblical passage except by the determination of the preacher, who pursues a personal agenda and then attributes it to the Holy Spirit. The text is a springboard. I have to say that I have some sympathy for anyone stuck in the depths of Leviticus. When faced with an unpromising passage, most preachers will wriggle, twist and turn in a game attempt to nourish the listeners. The virtuosi may even pull four-and-twenty blackbirds out of a forlorn text. Nevertheless, we feel that it must normally be possible to move from passage to message in a controlled and responsible way.

In addressing this issue I am not assuming that there is only one 'right answer' hidden in the passage, nor am I ignoring the considerable freedom, imagination and creativity demonstrated by the writers of the New Testament when they handled the Old Testament Scriptures. There must be always be a place for the individual to reflect on Scripture and come away with a message which is idiosyncratic, bearing all the marks of his or her distinctive way of looking at the world. In fact, this situation is probably the right place to begin.

LOOKING AT MYSELF

In Exodus 34.29–35 we read about Moses climbing the mountain of the Lord and speaking with God face to face, as friend to friend. When he came down from the heights the people were alarmed and backed away because his face was radiant, even though at first he was unaware of this. When he had finished speaking to them, he put a veil over his face. And after this, whenever he entered the

Lord's presence to speak with him, Moses removed the veil until he came out. And when he came out and told the Israelites what he had been commanded, they saw that his face was radiant.

This strange and compelling story has a lot to tell us about preaching. Most of us would like to be the man or the woman with the shining face. We would like people to recognize that we had been in the presence of God and were coming with a word from him which was piping hot out of the oven: 'they realized that he had spoken with the Lord'. What's even better is that Moses himself seems not to have been aware of his appearance. He had no need to avert his gaze self-effacingly when the Israelites said, 'Lovely sermon, vicar'. He did not need to mumble, 'Well, one does one's best', or even, less modestly but perhaps more honestly, 'Yes, I thought it was pretty good, too'. Without knowing it, he had become the mouthpiece of God, and the glory came off him with such brilliance that the Israelites couldn't bear to look. But, quite simply, the shining face could not (and cannot) be faked or kept in a jar by the vestry door. Moses' face shone because he had spent time in the presence of God and because God had spoken to him 'as a man speaks with his friend'.

This story highlights a number of significant features about preaching:

- Preaching is as much about listening as it is about speaking. Whatever the subject of the conversation between Moses and God, it's not likely to be covered by knocking up a few thoughts based on the newspaper or the Nine O'Clock News.
- The story asserts that God does still speak if you listen keenly enough. Moses heard an authentic word; he may have chiselled out the tablets himself – but the finger that wrote on them was God's.
- In a world where many have given up on preaching and seem to assume that the human concentration-span has shrunk to that of a lobotomized gnat, the story encourages us to go on speaking out of the *overflow* of our dialogue with God. We preach in the faith that people will recognize his accents, and acknowledge the origin of what we say.

There is nothing more important than climbing the mountain and listening in silence.

I know for myself that there is an excitement about getting to grips with a passage. I want to consult the commentaries, start jotting down ideas and collecting illustrations. The temptation to begin all this frantic but fulfilling activity with a quick prayer, and then to *get on*, is overwhelming.

But ... there is nothing more important than climbing the mountain and listening in silence.

Even when reading a book like this there may be an impatience with the author's wish to make his pious point before we can move on to the practical possibilities. 'Let's take the bit about prayer for granted. Let's see what he has to say about different techniques for getting a message out of a passage.' But ... there is nothing more important than climbing the mountain and listening in silence. Why am I labouring this point? Because I know that this is the part I most easily neglect. Forty days and forty nights listening is a severe test for someone who never did see much value in deferred gratification.

So, first of all and above all, listen in silence and let God speak.

It is presumably to encourage silent listening that Fred Craddock advises the preacher not to touch the commentaries at the beginning of this period of listening, praying and reflecting. This is time with God. The conversations with Calvin, Matthew Henry, William Temple, Sanders, Barrett, Brown and Dunn can wait for a moment. This is the time when we can allow the passage to speak to our whole person. We can take time to let powerful images or scenes in a story work on our imagination. In our mind's eye we can transpose ourselves into the passage.

I have found it helpful during this period to focus on two questions in particular. The first is borrowed from Craddock and asks, 'Where am I standing in the text?'

Many Bible texts invite us to identify with characters – we can hardly help doing it. In fact, I've just identified the preacher with Moses. But it is always worth asking, 'With whom am I identifying in this passage?'

As an exercise, read the story of Peter and John at the Beautiful Gate in Acts 3.1–10. As you get into the scene, ask yourself, 'What kind of message is beginning to emerge? How am I going to preach this?' Now pause and ask yourself, 'From what standpoint am I going to preach? Where am I standing in this passage?'

I suggest this exercise because Craddock goes on to warn us: 'Preachers tend to gravitate to the best seats in the text'. When I was preparing a sermon on the Peter and John passage, I began (predictably) to explore the role of the Church in identifying those in need on its doorstep, ministering to them, offering them the riches of Christ, etc., etc. The sermon was well on the way to a first draft when the thought occurred to me, 'Who says you're Peter and John? Who says you're not the crippled man?' As a result the whole sermon changed direction. We naturally align ourselves with Jesus or the apostles. Craddock observes that many congregations must sigh, 'Today our minister is Jesus and we are the Pharisees – *again*'. Now, without cheating, where do you stand in the story of the 'woman of the city' in Luke 7.36–50? With Jesus, being accepting and forgiving? With Simon the Pharisee, shocked, stiff, condemning? With the woman, tearful, repentant, adoring? Or with the other guests?

The second question is, 'What questions does this passage ask of *me*?' Sermon construction begins with personal exposure to God through the passage. As we listen, we are addressed and stopped in our tracks. This is why Walter Burghardt maintains that the sermon begins in the preacher as worshipper: 'It has its roots in the preacher's prayer life. And it begins when I preach to myself.' The preacher dare not read the passage looking for bits which will apply to others:

Not therefore, 'Here is an ideal application for the selfish in the parish, for the lukewarm, for the sex-crazed, for today's entrepreneur, the megabucks addict, the "me" generation.' No, with the toll-collector in the temple, I dare not even lift my eyes to heaven, but beat my breast: 'God be merciful to me *the* sinner' (Luke 18.13).[2]

> Read Romans 13.8–14, a reading often set for the beginning of Advent. What questions does the text ask of you?

I tried this exercise with a group of Methodist local preachers. The questions which emerged were: Am I loving? Am I capable of loving everyone like that? Am I awake or am I a dozy, half-asleep Christian? Am I neutral and disengaged? Or involved and engaged? Have I realized that there's a war on? Am I a hypocrite or real? Is Christ still the focus of my Christian life or have I lost him somewhere along the line? These questions seem a very good place to begin.

LOOKING AT THE PASSAGE

I have suggested that we should begin by putting ourselves under the spotlight. However, this does not mean that we are only concerned with what the passage has to say to us: other concerns are equally involved. When searching for a message to preach, I have found it helpful to look at the text from three different perspectives.

1 What is the main point?

It is a mark of respect to the text to ask what is its main point – the conclusion to which the argument is addressed, the climax of the narrative, the demand to which every aspect of the passage leads, the truth to which the images and illustrations point, and so on. This focus on the main point of the passage will help us faithfully to expound what the passage says, and will prevent our using it as a pretext or an excuse for saying something that we wanted to get off our chest all along. Many preachers argue that you should try to frame that main point in a single sentence, preferably as a positive statement, not as an exhortation. They believe that it is then more likely to come out as good news. Taking as an example the story of the ten lepers in Luke 17.11–19, the main point should be framed as a statement – 'Sometimes the most unexpected people are those who act rightly towards God' – rather than an exhortation –

'Remember to thank God for all his goodness'.

Peter Adam goes one step further: he works on a distillation of the passage and then constructs what he calls a 'ministry sentence' which focuses the direction of the sermon. 'It summarizes my ministry to the congregation, is expressed in terms of the expected response and includes an element of appeal or challenge.' For example, his ministry sentence for 1 Corinthians 6.12–20 is, 'Flee immorality!'; and for Galatians 4.12–5.1, 'Stand firm in freedom!'[3] It's worth bearing this advice in mind – though I have my reservations about trying to apply the technique indiscriminately, as the next point will illustrate.

2   Where is the passage going?

Not every passage stays still. Sometimes, it is true, there is one main point which can be illustrated from a dozen different angles. But equally, there are many occasions when the passage moves onwards. In such cases, the distinctive voice of Scripture may not be the static picture seen from several different angles, but the moving video. Now we need to ask a different question: 'What is *the movement* of the passage?' A psalm may shift from grief to praise; a set of proverbs may throw together contrasting, even contradictory, certainly bewildering, assertions, all sounding equally confident. Parables often move in this disturbing way, and therefore their force may be lost by turning them into three or four static pictures. At this point we need to ask, 'What is the movement of the passage? And what is it trying to do?' Now we are concentrating on the function of the passage and, in a sensible way, trying to reproduce that purpose and function in the sermon. Very often, movement and function are interwoven with form and mood. We will then want to recreate something of the form and mood of the passage, to ensure that the message we preach has not changed the basic thrust of the text by resetting it in a form and mood which work against those of the original (see pages 77 and 83 for some examples of this).

3   Where is the point of contact?

Studying the Bible in order to find advice and direction for contemporary living is, at first sight, an extraordinary thing to do.

It's a very old book and the world it describes is long gone. Nevertheless, I try to let this ancient text speak to me and speak for me, because it is Scripture and because I assume a common humanity with the people who lived in that time. I can trust that their experiences of life and of the ways of God are not entirely alien to mine. Moreover, behind the world of the Scriptures is a God who is alive and is eternal and, since he does not change, there is a good chance that I can find something which will speak directly to my world. If the world of the text can be an opening into the ways of God, it makes sense to search the passage for a dynamic analogy, for some point of contact between that world and this. I try to match the world and the message of the text against my world, my situation, my problems, needs, aspirations. Believing that the idea of an analogy is not an entirely foolish one, I look for parallels, for spiritual principles which are embodied within the passage and which may have their equivalents within my world.

The dangers of this approach are obvious. Considerable care must be exercised when trying to expose the principle which lies just beneath the specific particulars of a biblical passage. And if exegesis is a risky business, then there is an equal danger in re-embodying that principle in a particular drawn from our world. Here more than anywhere, the preacher needs to behave responsibly. For example, what might be the present-day equivalent of 'the elements of this world' in the epistle to the Colossians? – or of 'meat offered to idols' in 1 Corinthians? The haste for a quick contemporary parallel may lead to our failure to read the text carefully, and to our being satisfied with one point of correspondence instead of searching for an adequate equivalent.

LOOKING AT THE LISTENERS

Very often the word that you must speak comes alive when you think yourself into the situation of the hearers. Haddon Robinson suggests that exegetical study starts to snap and crackle when it is subjected to three questions: 'What does this mean?'; 'Is it true?'; 'What difference does it make?'[4] I think this advice is very helpful. When I am trying to hear how a passage might be addressing our world, I ask myself four questions.

1   What human need is this passage addressing?

Here we need to go back to our first encounter with the passage, when we tried to read it faithfully and imaginatively, when we looked for the 'surprise' in the text. To what element in the human condition does this passage's surprise speak? The sermon will then address human hopes or longings, desires to be different, safe or loved.

2   Where's the problem?

It is odd how often the most fruitful ground in which to dig is among the difficulties which the passage raises. We ask, 'What is there in the text which someone in the congregation might find difficult to accept? At what point will they say, "Well, it doesn't seem like that to me"?' The sermon has a chance to address the unspoken questions, such as: 'Yes, I'd like it to be so, but is it true? And is it true just as you say? With no qualifications at all? Are you hearing my objections?' We need to cultivate the devil's advocate within us – the voice which says, 'That's all very well but ...'. Then the sermon grows out of the tension between the question, 'Is it true?', and our responsibility to test what the passage seems to claim.

3   Yes, but whatever does that mean?

Here we need to heed the plain, blunt-speaking, awkward customer within ourselves who demands Straight Answers to Life's Problems. Give room to the practical, no-nonsense character who says, 'This is a very difficult idea. It may be interesting to theologians and other impractical people, but I haven't got a clue what you're talking about.' This question invites a sermon which will first explain and clarify, and then try to show the relevance of the idea and communicate something of its emotional force and power. A sermon which aims at clarification is not only about making things clear but also about helping the congregation to see how important or precious the idea is. The 'purpose' of Christian truth is never just to make us better informed.

4 What difference does it make?

Some teaching may be very clear – indeed it may be too clear for comfort – but may still leave the congregation untouched. Many Christian truths are like the command to love one another. They invite the response, 'What's new? So what? Who cares?' – or even an impatient, 'Yes, yes, yes'. When dealing with a truth which is failing to get a purchase on the listeners' imaginations, the preacher is challenged to bring it alive and embody it, to enflesh the general principle with examples and instances.

> At the risk of irritating you, I want to suggest an example for you to work on. Read the story of the wise men in Matthew 2. Apply the four questions above to the passage. Listen to the answers given by your imaginary congregation. How would you express them?

Here are some possibilities.

1 *What human need is the passage addressing?* The sense of my life as a journey, of travelling in search of a deeper knowledge of God, looking for the Christ-child, setting out on a quest; a journey outward but also a journey inward. My longing to 'come home'.

2 *Where's the problem?* In my life, is there too much travelling and no arriving? Is there a journey's end to come home to? Is the star a will-o'-the-wisp? Why do I always end up at Herod and never at the baby?

3 *What does it mean?* What on earth am I to make of the star? Have I got to study *Amateur Astronomer* to appreciate it? I need help to understand what's going on. What is the point of the gifts? Are they tributes brought by devotion? Or are the wise men astrologers laying down their arts at Christ's feet? Is this a story about the light of Christ banishing the darkness?

4 *What difference does it make?* So it's about fulfilment of

prophecy – but that means nothing to me. How will it affect my life? And if it's the 'manifestation of Christ to the Gentiles', so what? If the gifts have symbolic significance, are they telling me any more than I know already about Christ as king, God and saviour? I knew that when I first learned 'We three kings of Orient are'.

Here's the raw material for more than one sermon. The activity also reminds us that there is more than one possible message in any text. Jerry Camery Hoggatt maintains that there is an 'I've got it!' of the passage and an 'I've got it!' of the sermon.[5] This neatly captures the sense of discovery and disclosure. You cannot mechanically excavate a preachable message by working through a checklist. I mistrust preaching by numbers, and hope that I have not given anyone the impression that the ideas listed above are anything more than suggestions of things you might try.

I feel the need to stress yet again the crucial importance of waiting on God. In this setting you, as potential preacher, begin a conversation with the passage, with God and with the congregation – a conversation in which you are an active participant but not the chairperson. A process begins of playing about (not a pejorative term) until an idea or an image or an angle grabs you. Then you shout 'Eureka!' And you have an idea of how the sermon will go.

4 Curbing a frisky theology

I once overheard a conversation between two colleagues which went
like this:

'I saw Fiona Brown the other day.'
'Oh really. I never got on with her. What did she say?'
'She asked to be remembered to you.'
'Amazing ...'
'And she wanted to know if you still talked as if your opinions were
an appendix to the Ten Commandments.'

We can daydream about Moses on the mountain asking God for a
loan of the chisel. 'These Ten Commandments are OK as far as
they go but you won't mind if I add a little something? You see,
basically, I don't much care for charismatics and I think everything
might be clearer if I spelled that out. I'm sure you agree. And
perhaps a word or two about quails. They give me indigestion.'
    This points up preaching's perilous potential for implying that
you are communicating the word of God while actually using it to
peddle your own views and prejudices. John Goldingay character-
izes this tendency as, 'Here are three points which I am prepared to
attribute to the Holy Spirit and inflict on you'. I have heard of a
preacher who regularly responded to comments about the length of
the sermon with the rejoinder, 'Well, I know the sermon was long
and had little to do with the Bible passage, but that was the word
which the Lord gave me'. This remark will trump anything you can
come up with, and leaves you without much to say in reply.
    Sometimes we are too quick to house-train the Bible. A friend
tells of a student who returned home in the vacation, having for the
first time begun to see the possibility of faith and to take the call of
Christianity seriously. He went to a Bible study at the vicarage, on

46

the annunciation story. He found the story strangely moving – Mary said yes to God, as we are all summoned to do. But foundered when the vicar applied the passage to the willingness to give generously to the fabric fund. You might think this was a justifiable application. To the student it domesticated God and trivialized Mary's response. (Or was the young man being overspiritual?)

Despite this cautionary tale, the fact is that we cannot keep ourselves completely out of the frame. Our sermons communicate our theology – that is, they embody particular ways of seeing the world, particular emphases and 'weightings', particular connections and concepts. Within the field of Christian doctrine there is ample scope for different patterns and maps. Like a flower-arrangement, it isn't just a matter of choice – a couple of roses with three red chrysanthemums – though the selection of ideas is clearly important. It is also a matter of arrangement – the roses at the front, the chrysanthemums behind.

In practice, most of us have 'favourite' truths and doctrines, though this may seem an odd way to put it. One bishop was fond of asking clergy at what point in the Lord's Prayer the words 'came alive' for them. I suppose the prudent answer was, 'From the Our Father right through to the Amen'– but for most there was a phrase which rang bells or was personally significant to them. This is not to say that the rest of the prayer was unimportant: just that specific phrases had a salience that others lacked. The same words are given different interpretations and different weightings by different people. Some phrases come from the heart; others are believed, but without ringing affirmation. Some are seen as crucial to the life of discipleship; others as part of orthodox belief, but hardly at the centre of life. Yet others may be primarily seen as problems and puzzles, giving rise to debate and study but not evoking devotion.

A ONE-SIDED CONVERSATION?

As a preacher, how can I deal with the problem of my theology determining what is allowed to emerge?

First of all, it's worth saying that this isn't entirely a problem. My spirituality is personal and idiosyncratic. I hope that it is recognizably Christian – but it is still a product of my own experience of God. It is an oddly shaped map: some elements may come into view only if I am quizzed on them; others I shall be quick to declare; yet others will be present because they are important to me – but just how important may not emerge until I find myself in a crisis. The elements in my creed have different 'weights'. My spirituality – that is, my concept of God, my experience of the life of faith, my understanding of what is important, my conclusions about the way in which God works and the way life is, my framework of doctrines and their interrelationships – ought to appear in my sermons. If it doesn't get preached at all, then I might as well be a committee report or a repetition of 'what the Church teaches' or a parrot ('This is what the Revd X says'). It is not going to be truth mediated through personality, and it will lack the distinctive packaging of grace and the gospel which is *me*. One of the more encouraging verses in this connection is Ephesians 3.10: 'through the church the multicoloured wisdom of God might be made known' (my paraphrase). Preachers can rejoice in the fact that their sermons reflect their personal spirituality. God is committed to his multicoloured wisdom.

I want to push this idea further. We are told that *eisegesis* – that is, reading things into a Bible passage – is a cardinal sin of the preacher. The ideal is *exegesis*, the careful, even painstaking, drawing out of the passage those things that are already there. This is worth saying, but it represents only part of what goes on when we prepare a sermon. In an engaging article on the role of imagination in preaching, Thomas Long argues that the jump from what the text *meant* to what the text *means* is not a step over a puddle but a leap across a chasm. The bridge from one side to the other must be supplied from somewhere – and that 'somewhere' is the preacher's imagination. Long suggests that, 'The connection between the ancient text and the contemporary world is not procedural but poetic, not mechanical but metaphorical'.[1] We do not need to be excessively suspicious of the preacher's creative imagination. I bring something of myself to the passage. What I read is filtered through my present understanding. A conversation takes place between myself and the passage. None of this should be taken to mean that preachers can treat the Bible like some sort of inkblot, reading into it whatever takes their fancy. But, as Long suggests, nor is the meaning of the passage lying there inert, waiting to be excavated. Rather, 'the interpreter brings together the two poles, the ancient text and the present situation, and allows the spark of imagination to jump between them'.[2]

When does 'the conversation' become a problem? When does it become so one-sided that the Bible is reduced to silence, while the preacher harangues the congregation? It is not easy to give a hard-and-fast rule, though I suspect that very often the congregation will spot what is happening before the preacher does. But something has clearly gone wrong when my assumptions dictate in advance what I shall hear and what I shall see in the Bible. Something has gone wrong when I fail to read what is as plain as it could possibly be, when Scripture loses the power to shock, surprise, change my perspective and challenge me to action, when I fail to read carefully, and rush on to make a cheap point (even if a true one) without listening. Like any conversation, courtesy requires it to be a two-way affair. If Scripture is not allowed to say everything it wants to say, we soon reach a point where God cannot surprise us with fresh truth.

MAP-MAKING FOR BEGINNERS

These considerations make it vital for preachers to be aware of the theology which they are preaching Sunday by Sunday. If you have a simple map of your theological fads and favourites you are better able to see if the 'message' that emerges from the text is legitimately present or is another example of your pet hate or love popping up in the most unlikely places. The map may help you to check if there is some other message hiding just out of sight, over-shadowed by the idea which naturally elbows its way to the front whenever you get yourself into a 'discerning a message' pose. It will also force you to compensate for your biases by having to take seriously doctrines and emphases which are not part of your natural repertoire. And in any case, it is never a bad thing to know consciously the kind of message which is coming across.

What each of us needs is a basic map of our theology, along with some idea of how it shows itself in our sermons. This could be a lifetime's work, and its production is certainly beyond the scope of this book and the capacity of the author. We can make a start, however, at a simpler level.

The Open University unit, *Man's Religious Quest*, used to pose three questions about any religious tradition: From what? By what? To what? Take a recent sermon and analyse its thought. How do you describe the human predicament? (i.e. from what must people be rescued?) How is the problem transformed? (i.e. by what means is the rescue achieved?) What form of hope is offered? (i.e. to what desirable state does the rescue lead?)

We might come at the issue from a different direction, by asking ourselves a series of questions:

- What are your major images of God? Does he appear as the disturber (a favourite image of David Jenkins, the former Bishop of Durham), or as a judge, or resident policeman? Is he primarily a lawgiver? Or Father Christmas? An impersonal force? Daddy?
- What images of Christ do you work with? A Christ of infinite love, care and patience for the lost and marginalized, the despised and the oppressed? A Christ with the whip of cords?
- What do you condemn? How do you describe sin? As rebellion? As an ignorant straying from the path? As being lost and far from home?
- Where is your emphasis on salvation and transformation? On the incarnation? The atonement? The resurrection? The presence and power of the Holy Spirit? The Bible? The sacraments?
- How do you characterize the life of faith? Basically as triumph? As a battle and a striving? Do you see doubt, and feelings of hopelessness, as normal parts of the Christian life, or do you set them outside the circle of authentic discipleship?
- As you study the sermon, if you had to choose a key phrase, term or image to describe the heart of your theological position as it is expressed, what would it be?
- What are the give-away lines which show more of what you like and dislike than you at first realize? Where do your sympathies lie? What phrases let the cat out of the bag?
- Is Christianity, for you, primarily a matter of private devotion and piety or does it affect the public domain? Will the 'answer' hinted at in your sermon turn the congregation inwards into the church and the home, or outwards to society? When you describe 'the change Christ makes', from where do you draw

your examples?

- Do you think Christianity is a matter of the head, the will or the heart? What is the role of emotions and feeling?
- Is Christianity about listening and learning from experience? Or is it about receiving and trusting what has been handed down to us – if necessary, in the teeth of experience?

These questions are not intended to direct you, even subtly, towards what I conceive to be the 'right' or approved positions. I think most of them, at some time or another, might legitimately be preached. Their purpose is to help you see more clearly the drift and tendency of your theological position; to help you dismount from the hobby horse and ensure that aspects of Christian truth which are not immediately congenial or natural to you are allowed their proper place in your preaching. Paul claimed that he had taught the whole counsel of God. This inventory, or something like it, may help us do the same.

AND JUST BENEATH THE SURFACE ...

I conclude this discussion with an example of how the map-making might work.

Below is a brief meditation, written for television – which ensures that it is short and fairly easy to analyse. It is on the multiplication of the loaves (John 6.1–13). The 'preacher' would not want it to be considered a fully fledged sermon. Your task is to analyse its basic theology.

The hillside became a picnic site. Five thousand and more sitting down in the heat of a Galilean afternoon. Reds, blues, greens, purples, tee shirts with dubious messages, sawn-off jeans, bare feet, bare midriffs and bare beer bellies. 'Phew, what a scorcher', the papers will say. Roll your trousers up. Pass the suntan lotion. Knot the corners of your handkerchief if you haven't got a hat. A vast field of colour, as far as you could see. Like the county show or a rock festival or a Classic FM concert. People sprawled out on the grass. A rainbow of human flowerbeds. Just the setting for a picnic. Except there was no food. They'd chased Jesus across the lake with such enthusiasm, they'd forgotten all about the Chablis and the smoked salmon. They'd even forgotten the phone number of Presto Pizza – delicious-dishes-delivered-directly-to-your-door.

Watch Jesus carefully. What will he say? Something sensible, no doubt. 'It's not the management's policy to compensate you for lack of forward planning. Nothing to do with me. God helps those who help themselves. You should have thought of that before now. What makes you think you're so special? If I rustle up some food, what's it worth? No such thing as a free lunch.' All reasonable things to say. So watch him. Just watch the grace of God in overdrive. 'He took the loaves, gave thanks, and gave the loaves to those sitting down. Then he did the same thing with the fish.' A little piece, a crumb, a morsel perhaps. A taste on the tongue. Not quite. He gave and gave and gave and gave and gave … On and on and on and on and on … It came pouring out of him. As much as they wanted. Abundant. Overflowing. A cornucopia of bread. An inexhaustible supply. This is the Christ who gives life as God gives life – extravagantly. The Christ who goes to a wedding, finds that they have run out of wine and produces 150 gallons. This is the divine Mozart spinning symphonies of bread from his finger-tips. A God of soft-centred chocolates by the crateful. Here on the hillside is the Creator, who says, 'Let there be bread', and there was bread. As much as they wanted. In the fifth row back somebody says, 'I only said I felt a bit peckish and all this bread fell on me.' 'Bread of heaven, feed me till I want no more!' Lord, I am bursting. Stop it! The lavish, unnecessary, limitless, superabundant generosity of Christ. God who doesn't know when to stop. Prodigal, spendthrift, lavish. This bounteous God. Just look at their faces. That's what I mean by grace.

And then Jesus said something astonishing. It was about the crumbs. The broken bits, the dropped bits, the too-small-to-eat bits; the bits that get lost in the grass. He said,

'Pick them up. I don't want a single fragment to be lost.'
That is fantastic. He wouldn't let anything be lost. So he
won't say to you and me, 'You're thick, you're ugly, you're
unemployed. You've got no talent, you've got no money.
Wrong colour, wrong accent. You cry too much, you smell,
you're too old. And you've made one mistake too many.' I
like him, this Christ who bothers about fragments, the
broken, fractured, useless, good-for-nothing pieces.

All I did was offer him my pain and confusion, my petti-
ness and unwillingness to forgive, my hesitant and faithless
prayers, my stammering and faltering speech, my plans and
projects, my abilities (such as they are). All I did was ask
that he would touch me with his Spirit. All I did was come
to his table with empty hands ... And he multiplied the
loaves and gave me grace on top of grace and filled me with
the Bread of Life.

I don't know what you have identified as the main ideas in this
piece. I think the controlling concept of the grace of God (the 'God
who doesn't know when to stop') is pretty obvious. I want just to
emphasize what I think is going on in the penultimate paragraph
('And then Jesus said something astonishing ...'), which illustrates
what I mean by a conversation with the text.

At first sight, the incident seems distant from the point which the
sermon makes. The story in John's gospel says nothing about 'the
Christ who bothers about fragments', except in the literal sense.
Where has this portrait of Christ come from if not from the
preacher's imagination? Furthermore, why has the sermon not
taken the obvious eucharistic line? – the 12 disciples look remark-
ably like forerunners of the Church, distributing the bread of life
from Christ's hands to the multitude; and the command to gather
up the fragments may be a hint at the precious nature of the
eucharistic bread and liturgical practice. Or, in topical mode, why
didn't the sermon deal with God's concern for every part of his
creation, the conservation of resources and a Christ who cares
about the way in which we handle the environment?

The answer is partly that the portrait of Christ who cares for the
fallen is a central element in the preacher's own theology. This idea
came more naturally to the surface than the alternatives. However,

the decision to take this particular line was not made wholly without reference to the passage. The text does exercise some control. First, in contrast to Mark, John *specifically does not say* that the 12 disciples distributed the bread. Next, in contrast to the discourse which follows, the miracle itself is centred on the multiplication of the loaves rather than on the bread of life. The preacher is thus freed to give full weight to the phrase 'as much as they wanted', and to focus on abundant grace as the theme of the sermon. Once the portrait of the prodigal, spendthrift Christ has been established, it is natural to ask about the place of the 'broken, fractured, useless, good-for-nothing' people within this scheme of divine generosity. The text offers a hint in the words 'that nothing be lost', a phrase which picks up John's eschatological use of 'lost' elsewhere in the gospel. That gives the preacher permission to explore his vision of Christ in the sentence, 'I like him, this Christ who bothers about fragments, the broken, fractured, useless, good-for-nothing pieces'.

The preacher thus finds this vision both within his own experience and within the passage. In courteous conversation with the passage, the preacher's imagination plays with the ideas it raises but is, at the same time, disciplined by it. As he explores the picture of Christ as one who cares for those who fall, the specific incident in John evokes a larger biblical truth. We are reassured that this is authentic Gospel. It may legitimately be found in the passage; it is not just a bright idea of the preacher. And in its turn, the specific incident contributes to and enriches the overall gospel picture of Christ. This is the kind of dialogue which I believe goes on when we engage with a biblical passage. It is vital to keep both partners talking and listening to each other.

5   Is it good news?

The gospel, by definition, is 'good news', and the preacher's message should reflect this. This may seem a very obvious point, and one hardly worth making – until you encounter people who say that they feel worse after having been to church than before they went. James Motl comments, 'Much of the preaching I hear sounds more like bad news than good news. That is to say, when preachers come down to talking about what they have seen and heard the message is more likely to be depressing than joyful.'[1]

Yet according to Mark, 'the common people heard Jesus gladly' (Mark 12.37), and this was not just because they stood a fair chance of seeing the tails of the scribes and Pharisees tweaked when he was around. The large crowds which chased after him (across the lake, in Solomon's portico, out into the desert) would hardly have bothered if what they heard was boring, irrelevant, insipid or trite. Jesus spoke with authority. His words carried conviction. He sounded as if he knew what he was talking about. When he asked his disciples if they were about to leave him, Peter replied, '"To whom should we go? You have the words of eternal life"' (John 6.68). Once people have seen something of that other world, once they have encountered the living God, they will walk 1,000 miles for another glimpse. To hear God speaking is good news.

And this is so, even if what we hear makes us quiver and tremble. Good news does not necessarily mean that the message is tailored to suit our preferences and prejudices. The preacher who concocts only what the congregation will swallow serves up tasteless pap. Salt that has lost its savour is good for gritting the roads, but not much else. On the whole, congregations do not pay their ministers to protect them from the real God. We need an understanding of sermons which allows them to be good news without turning them into yet another example of the need to 'feel good' at all times.

WHEN IS A SERMON BAD NEWS?

I can think of several factors which make a sermon bad news.

The tone of the sermon

We don't like being browbeaten or nagged. Sermons which scold are a major switch-off. The preaching of judgement does not have to sound moaning, whingeing and griping. Black preachers, the saying goes, sound 'fiery glad'; white preachers just sound 'fiery mad'. There is a standard sermon for Christmas which berates people for not coming to church during the rest of the year. It is a sure way of turning people off for another 12 months, and fits awkwardly with the warmth of the carol:

> Now may Mary's son who came
> so long ago to *love* us,
> lead us all with *hearts aflame*
> unto the *joys* above us.

The effect of the sermon

Being made to feel guilty about everything is really bad news, *if there is no way to deal with the guilt*. One man spoke to me of what he called 'the divine ho-hum'. 'Whatever I do', he said, 'I am left with Jesus' words about unprofitable servants. I say, "Look, Lord, I've tried. And I did manage to do this reasonably well. What do you think?" And the Lord says, "Ho-hum". It's so demoralizing.' A friend confided, 'Most of the time I pray, "O God, give us a break"'. Most of the time she felt bad enough without the sermon making her feel a total failure as a human being. It is one of the marks of the servant of the Lord that she does not snap the bruised reed or snuff out the smouldering wick. Feeling guilty is a very unproductive emotion, and the lifestyle which flows from it is usually unattractive and has little to do with the freedom which the gospel brings.

The preacher's view of us

The preacher's view of the congregation is obviously a key element
in whether the sermon will sound like good news. The content of
the message may be impeccable, but it will be heard negatively if we
feel that the preacher doesn't like us very much. We feel uneasy if
we sense that what drives the preacher is *disapproval* of the contemporary world rather than a desire to offer Christ. Impatience with
ordinary people and their funny little ways goes down badly with
us. If my life and the world in which I live is constantly rubbished,
it is small wonder that I react badly to the message.

Our impression of the preacher

There are preachers who seem too holy for mere mortals. A
message delivered by a super-saint will not communicate good news
because we will be sure that it is beyond us. We find it hard to hear
a preacher who doesn't know what it is like to fail, or to doubt: we
need to see something of the humanity behind the uniform. On the
other hand, we will have problems with good news which does not
seem aware of the world we live in. If the preacher never seems to
have experienced pain, has never had to cope with money problems, teenage children, stress at work or difficult relationships,
then how can we be sure that the solutions he or she proclaims will
match up to our problems? If preachers seem to have come off a
different planet, then the message is likely to seem weak, insipid or
vacuous.

The picture of God

What kind of God are we left with when the sermon is over? Feeling
that God dislikes us (which isn't the same as realizing that we are
under judgement) is not good news. Nor do we respond to a God
who demands worship as if he needed to be constantly congratulated
like an insecure managing director. A God who is bad-tempered, or
petty, spitefully set on getting his own back or obtaining his pound of
flesh is a distortion of the Christian God. There is all the difference
in the world between 'these are people under the wrath of God', and
'these are people for whom Christ died'. The latter fits better with

the Christ who was always to be found at parties and had the reputation for being a 'gluttonous man and a winebibber'. In the novel, *Bevis, a Boy*, the main character looks at a picture of the crucifixion and comes to the conclusion that he loves Jesus and hates God. Preaching which presents the atonement as anything other than the result of God's love is disastrously inadequate. In these subtle (and not so subtle) ways, the sermon can distort good news by projecting the preacher's own hang-ups.

The logic of the sermon

Sermons have a shape and a direction; they are designed according to a plan. The classic good-news sermon states a problem and names the grace of God as its solution. Those who listen hear their condition described with accuracy yet with sympathy; and they see how God acts in response, with grace and love. Unfortunately, many sermons appear to be structured according to a different pattern.

For example, some sermons moralize. But it is dispiriting to be subjected to a list of virtues and exhorted to reproduce them. Virtues are the results of being touched by grace, not a way of achieving it. Diderot said, 'Virtue is praised but hated. People run away from it for it is ice-cold and in the world you must keep your feet warm.' Even being confronted with Christ as our example can be a demoralizing experience. It is as if the preacher was saying, 'Try to jump as far as Jonathan Edwards'. The only answer to this is, 'I can't. I can't.' The list of virtues in Galatians 5.22–3 is specifically described by Paul as 'the harvest of the Spirit', not a syllabus for super-saints.

Other sermons are heavy on the analysis of the problem and easy on the solution. There is nothing quite like hammering the evils of modern society, in the style of Disgusted of Tunbridge Wells. You can really get your teeth into consumerism, the culture of violence, the media, materialism and the pursuit of sexual gratification. And after all this, somehow there isn't enough time for the good news, so you have to end with a quick summary statement ('God overcomes all this in the cross' – 'What? Did I miss something?'), or a general exhortation ('So let us all resolve, this Easter, to …'). But the congregation are left feeling as if they had gone to the doctor, got an extensive diagnosis and left without the prescription. Where was the good news?

These are some of the ways in which what was intended to be good news can come across as bad news. Before we move on, it might be useful to attempt the following task. You have decided to preach against the National Lottery (whether wisely or unwisely doesn't matter for the purposes of the exercise). What sort of points might you make? Is it possible to construct a sermon which doesn't sound like Victor Meldrew? Can you avoid falling into the traps set out above? Can the sermon contain any place for 'naming God's grace'?

These are some of the points you might choose to make (though some of them are a sermon in themselves!):

- Mention some plus points: concede that the National Lottery brings a great deal of excitement, and even produces a sense of togetherness (three-quarters of the nation are watching TV together); it also brings colour into drab lives.
- Mention some problems (but without undue moralizing): people spend money they can ill afford; it can lead to a kind of addiction, and so on.
- Look at the world-view implied by the Lottery. First, that the world is run by luck, or chance (or astrological mumbo-jumbo in the form of Mystic Meg). Second, there is an underlying assumption that money will solve most problems. Yet as Christians we believe that God is in control of our world, and that we should be content whatever our lot (Phil. 4.12); also that this same God chose poverty so that we might be truly rich.
- Explore the theology behind the National Lottery prayer: 'I know I'm a sinner, but make me a winner'. This recognizes that no one *deserves* the jackpot ... but occasionally you get something you don't deserve. Here is an opportunity to speak about the grace of God who gives generously whether we deserve it or not.

59

AND NOW FOR THE GOOD NEWS ...

If we accept Motl's comment, 'Much of the preaching I hear sounds more like bad news than good news', then what can preachers do to ensure that the criticism is not true of their sermons?

One helpful move might be to mark the bits of good and bad news in a particular sermon. Take the script of the sermon, set one emphasis against the other and then consider the totals. Even this exercise might not tell the whole story: an item which counts as 'bad news' might be presented with such power that it outweighs eight 'good news' items. The tone of a section may colour the whole piece or an especially vivid illustration may leave troubling images in the mind. So it is worth trying to assess the likely impact of each element. I heard of an address at a carol service which began by referring to two recent deaths and to the massacre at Dunblane. We need to balance the loads: an enormous suitcase of disaster and calamity in one hand cannot be balanced by a paper bag of joy in the other. Carrying such unequal loads merely gives you backache.

A second strategy involves the preacher's own spiritual experience. A preacher's preparation ought to include sitting down with the Bible passage and looking for the evidence of God's grace within the text. This activity cues the preacher towards grace, making it less likely that the sermon will highlight law, judgement or morality to the exclusion of forgiveness or freedom in the Spirit. The exercise becomes even more personal when preachers ask God to help them recognize areas of their own life where God's grace can be discerned. There is a good chance that the congregation will overhear snatches of that conversation in the sermon, and thereby catch the sense of sins forgiven and a heart strangely warmed. If the passage overflows with good news for the preacher, then, when it is preached, it will probably sound like good news to the congregation.

YOU GENERATION OF VIPERS!

You can't leave out all reference to sin and judgement. Preachers who never touch on these topics would be distorting the Christian faith. We know that all is far from well in the garden, even if the hymn does go on and on about all things bright and beautiful.

I begin by making the obvious points that preaching judgement is not the same as being bad tempered, and when we speak of sin we would do well to use 'we' rather more than 'you'. Luther's comment, 'When God wishes to heal, he first batters to pieces', may seem an unpromising contribution to the discussion but, even if he was right, we do not have to sound as if we are enjoying the prospect of others being battered. John Stott writes, 'We should speak of hell only in tears'. In fact, Luther's words remind us that the purpose of the battering is that God should *heal*. The good news contains a sombre assessment of the plight of humanity in order that it may move on to glad tidings of great joy. We need to keep that balance. We do not need to launch too many lightning bolts from the pulpit. It is enough faithfully to present the sober facts of the human predicament, and then to trust that an encounter with the terror and the glory of the living God will bring its own conviction of sinfulness.

How is it possible to avoid sounding 'preachy' and superior? Perhaps the key here lies in identifying with the congregation. Thorwald Lorenzen puts it this way: 'This is why love is necessary for preaching. God knows us because he loves us and the preacher will only discern the real questions of his congregation if he loves his hearers'.[2] A curate once began to visit a young couple in his parish who were expecting their first child. The curate was conscientious and disciplined in his pastoral care, but the couple were fairly typical young professionals, friendly enough to the clergyman as a person but without much interest in his spiritual wares. In due course the child was born, but soon became seriously ill and died. The curate was deeply upset by this and visited the couple to bring some kind of comfort to them. To his distress he was unable to say anything, but just sat in their living room crying. He left feeling a complete failure as a priest. To his amazement the couple came to church the following Sunday. 'I don't understand it', he said. 'When you needed me most I had nothing to give you.' The couple replied, 'But you gave us everything you had.' Congregations ask, 'Where does this preacher stand?' And the answer had better be, 'Like Christ, down in the Jordan with everyone else'. A preacher who is at one with people in their pain, failure and waywardness will be heard as the bringer of good news even on those occasions when he or she needs to rebuke or reproach.

A key factor in preaching good news lies in the preacher's authenticity, in the capacity to present a message that is real. It is easy to do no more in the pulpit than shuffle a well worn pack of cards, laying them out in different sequences and arranging them in pretty patterns. One preacher said that the finest compliment he had ever received was, 'You cut the crap'. The sermon is good news when it touches reality, when it deals with deeply felt emotions and when it opens up the spiritual dimension of our existence. Then people get the sense that God is real and is speaking to them. And that is good news precisely because the play-acting is over and the action has begun. Charades are fun, but are no substitute for real living. Aslan may be terrifying, but at least he's not a stuffed lion (or a donkey in a lion-skin – as C. S. Lewis's *The Last Battle* reveals).

This is a plea for reality in the pulpit. Sermons are real when there is genuine engagement with the problems of life, when the preacher speaks out of his or her own experience of God and the struggles of the life of faith without disparaging either. Trust and empathy are awakened when people recognize their pain in someone else. Even a psalm of complaint may be heard as good news precisely because it acknowledges the way we sometimes feel. 'A disembodied preacher cannot credibly proclaim the incarnate Christ … No preacher can grab us by the entrails who is not in touch with his or her own fundamental humanity.'[3] This means that the sermon must face issues honestly, speaking 'what we know, not what we ought to say'. Alongside such straight talking, we ought also to proclaim a message which has the ring of truth and possibility about it. Sermons are intended to give answers – though that doesn't mean that they ought to sidetrack hard questions in order to peddle slick pick-me-ups. The theology of the cross is about the God who is with me in the darkness and who will one day bring me to new life. No matter how incoherent the situation, there's got to be some loving in it somewhere, even if a proper sensitivity to other people's pain stops us from being too strident about proclaiming it. Christian hope is thoroughly realistic. It accepts that things are bad and does not pretend otherwise – but it refuses to leave people in the pit. It isn't vacuous optimism or making the best of a bad job. At the end of the day, the gospel is about resurrection, new life and joy. These are the solid realities of the faith. Proclaimed with integrity, there is no better news.

PART THREE

Finding a Voice

6 Learning from the experts

Night after night, every week of the year, somewhere in Britain someone will get up and hold forth to a congregation which has probably had a little too much to drink. The night club comedian, the after-dinner speaker and the TV comic have to be masters of their craft. The laws of natural selection operate unforgivingly: if you get it right, you get paid and may get to do it again; if you get it wrong, you die. Of course, Chrysostom, Augustine, Luther, Wesley and Spurgeon knew their art, and we can learn a lot from them. But the successful stand-up comic in a working men's club is no amateur either. He or she has managed to survive in an environment that would destroy the average preacher. Only rarely will a congregation shout, 'Get off', or throw hymn books. Whatever the comedian knows, it has been learned in a hard school – and is not to be despised. Can we learn anything?

I am not pretending that preaching and telling jokes have much in common. Preaching is a spiritual task; the comedian is in the entertainment business. Something desperate happens to churches when they are hellbent on entertainment. One American church put out a mailshot headed, 'Ten top reasons for coming to our church', and offering free coffee and drinks, and promises that you'll be out in an hour with plenty of time to enjoy the rest of the day, that you can leave your wallet at home, that you'll be allowed to blend in and remain anonymous, and that they will never visit you. The saying, 'He who marries the spirit of this age will find himself a widower in the next', is a straight warning against cheapening the preaching task.

Nevertheless, the three types of 'preacher' mentioned above intersect with a wide cross section of society. They touch the worlds of the club, the pub, the students' union, the formal banquet, the TV dinner. Those who speak in these situations possess an expertise from which most preachers can learn. I know I can't adopt without qualification the techniques of the media masters – but I find myself admiring their skills even while reserving judgement on their values. And I often find myself wistfully wishing that I could reproduce half their impact in the service of the Gospel. To parody William Booth, why should the Devil have all the best lines? It will take a rare arrogance to say that they can teach us nothing. After all, it was Jesus who talked about the children of this world being wiser than the children of light.

We also need to take account of a second feature of contemporary culture. We live in a media-saturated world, and within that world of tabloid journalism, television, film, radio, the Internet and computer games, television is the king. Forty million people watch television every day for two to three hours (the statistics vary according to which expert you listen to, but the figures are always astronomically high). We can't pretend it isn't there: no book on preaching can afford to ignore the context in which we preach.

Unfortunately, in a society dominated by television the sermon has a hard time. Television is good at depicting conflict and polarization, and is happier stereotyping than reproducing the untidiness of real life. I remember a television interview when Paul Eddington, a wonderful actor coping impressively with a disfiguring skin disease, said to the interviewer, 'Let's not make this a TOT piece' (i.e. Triumph Over Tragedy). On television even education has to be 'infotainment'. Balanced reflection makes producers nervous, hesitation looks as if you've forgotten your lines or have something to hide, long silences are death. Much television recalls Paul's warning about a society with itching ears – but, like it or not, television affects everything we touch.

So what can we learn from the communication experts? What can we learn from Ben Elton, Jasper Carrott, Billy Connolly, Jo Brand and Victoria Wood? What can we learn from television – the news, the soaps and the advertisements?

LEARNING FROM THE TV

We can live in the contemporary world

The comedian and the after-dinner speaker know the world of

their audience. This is the world of the union bar, the Rotary Club, the amateur pigeon fanciers of West Moseley's annual awards dinner, or the Greesely and Wimblingwolds working men's club. But, significantly, it is also the world of television. The speech will not be restricted to the local: it will range across what is now our common culture, the world of *The Big Match*, *EastEnders*, *Cracker*, *They Think it's All Over* and *Friends* (by the time you read this, the list may already have a dated air).

I have written as if this world were that of the Marsh Arabs – a culture which the missionary would do well to work on. But the world of television, along with the car radio and tabloid journalism, is *our* world, not that of a strange tribe. It is certainly the world of our Sunday congregations. Television represents the environment in which the Church lives, and within which preaching takes place. This is the world that people bring with them to church. Some will prefer *The Antiques Roadshow* and *Gardeners' World* to *Red Dwarf* and *Eurotrash* – but there will still be many programmes that most will watch from time to time. These provide a stock of shared information and experiences, a common culture. Television also forms the congregation's expectations of what counts as credible communication, and may even affect listening habits (the apparent ability to do four things at once while the TV twinkles in the corner) and attention spans (the viewer's tendency to zap between channels).

I am impressed by the ease with which the communications experts move around this world. Most popular speakers have an extraordinary feel for where the audience is: rapport is high because they live in the world which television provides. Their material is up to date. Like the panel on *Have I Got News for You*, they have read this week's papers. They know this world intimately, and don't give themselves away by making silly mistakes. I realize that the knowledge required to impress, say, a student audience is different from that needed for an elderly congregation. However, whatever the specific audience, popular speakers know the culture of those to whom they speak. We would do well to copy their example.

I knew one minister who took two daily papers all his life: one was a so-called quality paper, the other a tabloid. It was one way of finding out what his congregation were thinking and of making sure that when he preached he wasn't just muttering to himself. In the spring of 1997, a number of bishops were given a quiz to test their street credibility. To his great credit, Bishop Michael Nazir-Ali came top, for being able, among other achievements, to say who the Spice Girls were and to name all five. And I was strangely heartened that the Archbishop of Canterbury understood a Radio One disc jockey's chant of 'Oooh ah Cantona!' and was able to relate it to footballer Eric Cantona.

We can observe the contemporary world

The first-class comedian or after-dinner speaker seems to possess a keener sight than most of us. Take this excerpt from a Victoria Wood script. You will recognize it as a parody of a typical TV chat show.

> *Joan*: And as Philippa climbs out of that piranha tank, I'm sure she won't mind if I let you into a little secret – she's actually into the fourth week of a very serious breakdown! Now it's over to Margery, who's been finding out what's available holiday-wise for those who aren't going abroad this summer. Hello, Margery, what's available holiday-wise for those who aren't going abroad this summer?
>
> *Margery*: Hello, Joan. Well, believe it or not but not every holiday-maker will be flying to Marbella or Alicante with a suitcase full of velour leisure shorts singing 'Y Viva Espana'.
>
> *Joan*: And why is that, Margery?
>
> *Margery*: Possibly because they don't know the words to the second verse, Joan.
>
> *Joan*: So a lot of people will be looking for a reasonably priced package in this country?
>
> *Margery*: That's right, Joan.
>
> *Joan*: OK – so I'm single, I don't have very much money, I can't afford to go abroad, I don't make friends easily. What can I do?
>
> *Margery*: Look, we had all this out in the wine bar ...

(*Realizes her mistake.*) Well, there's lots of alternatives available, Joan, the cheapest being a two-week conservation holiday in the West Midlands dragging old bedsteads out of the Grand Union Canal and living on pulses.[1]

We might note the amount of specific reference in this piece. It represents careful listening and looking. In fact, the observation is so accurate that we wince as we laugh. 'Dragging old bedsteads out of the Grand Union Canal and living on pulses' is a whole lot more graphic than the generalized 'two-week conservation holiday'. 'Flying to Marbella or Alicante with a suitcase full of velour leisure shorts' is much sharper than 'Going on holiday'. Sermons can learn from the technique.

We can reframe and reinterpret the contemporary world

Comedians offer us a new slant on familiar things. In this sense, they work in the same area as the preacher, since both help us to see the everyday in a new light. Ben Elton once produced an extended monologue on going to the post office. He contrasted the new post office, which offers you only one queue to join, with the old type which offered a queue per window. The old post office was a place of excitement and frustration, of strategic manoeuvres, triumph and despair. The triumph came from constantly moving from the queue you were in to another one which, though longer, was moving faster. The despair came after you'd done this several times and got stuck behind two Swedish students trying to send a package to Stockholm by the cheapest method, or a pensioner getting £10-worth of television stamps and three postal orders. Elton managed to describe this scene in a frenetic eight minutes of graphic description. At the end of the sequence I thought, 'Why am I laughing so much?' The answer lay in the shock of recognition. Elton had shown the audience something familiar but had turned it on its side, reframing it as Mission Impossible, high adventure, a quest, with tasks to be achieved and ordeals to be overcome.

A quirky view of life is one of the gifts of the comedian. Take just two examples. First, an after-dinner speaker who asks why Concorde has frosted glass in the loo windows: 'You're thousands of feet above the ground, flying at the speed of sound, the outside temperature's below freezing. And there's frosted glass in the loo windows. Who's going to look in?!' Secondly, Douglas Adams, who has invented a unit of measurement, the nad. A nad is the distance between the ticket machine at the entrance or exit of a multi-storey car park and the tips of your outstretched fingers: it is exactly 18.4 centimetres. The comedian peers into the depths of ordinary life and then helps us to see it in fresh ways. This is not a bad way of describing one of the tasks of the preacher.

The everyday life which the preacher has to interpret is bigger than the world as presented by television, but it certainly includes it. The preacher ought not to pretend it isn't there. One of the effects of national television is that what it covers becomes centre stage for that period. News items are given weight and importance merely by being selected for report. Reporters who comment from the very spot communicate a sense of immediacy and urgency: 'It is happening at this very moment here in Washington' (library pictures of the White House). Congregations are immersed in this coverage. They will value some acknowledgement of the fact that 'something big happened this week'. They may be looking for help with how to interpret the event, how to incorporate it into a Christian world-view, and how to communicate their response to others. It is interesting to see how the BBC's *Thought for the Day* (on Radio 4) has evolved from a devotional reflection into an interpretative comment on a topical issue. For the preacher, this is not the same as letting the transient concerns of the media control the word of God. After all, Jesus himself was not averse to referring to the news: 'Those eighteen who died when the tower in Siloam fell on them – do you think they were more guilty than all the others living in Jerusalem?' (Luke 13.1–5).

FORMAT AND FOCUS

The masters of communication employ a variety of techniques, most of which can be borrowed by the preacher.

Story

Comedians like Jasper Carrott and Peter Ustinov tell stories all the time. Their material is organized around plot and character. The conventional joke works swiftly towards its punch line. What strikes me about the story-telling comedian is the time he or she is prepared to take over the story for its own sake, and the loving attention given to detail which is itself milked for humour. A serious point can be carried if it is embedded in a loosely linked string of stories and one-liners. Peter Moloney is currently a highly successful after-dinner speaker. He often likes to incorporate a serious message through jokes: one of his recurring themes is how hard it is for people to communicate effectively. 'Words get in the way,' he groans, as if in real pain. 'Take the lodger who complained there wasn't a plug in the bath. "Of course there isn't," replied his landlady. "The bath's not electric."'[2]

Preachers have known for centuries that people remember stories, but still naturally turn to precepts. This is odd when we remember that we follow a master who spent much of his time speaking in parables.

Human interest

People are interesting. Knowing this, the tabloid newspapers frame their reports around personalities. Almost at random, I turn to a page in a national daily: one story begins, 'A British wife has been murdered in a jail while on a sex visit to her killer husband'. On the same page a headmistress comments on school league-tables, leading to the headline, 'Girls will stop rot in Britain'. We are intrigued by the woman who kept an unexploded bomb as an ornament on her mantelpiece for 20 years, not realizing the danger. We want to know more about the man who rang his wife and asked her to come and pick him up from a party because he'd had too much to drink. (Apparently she said, 'No, take a bus'. So he went to the bus station and drove one away. He was four times over the limit and was jailed for five months!) But there again, we are intrigued by the man who had two sons, the woman who lost a coin, the steward who got the sack and the householder who decided to hold a dinner party.

The specific

The general and the abstract have to struggle for our attention; the specific and the concrete stand a better chance of holding us. The specific means talking about detail. Here is Victoria Wood, on the problems of the Health Service:

> Mrs Smith? Yes, I'm looking at the figures now – the waiting-list situation – 15 months for a tonsillectomy, three years for a hip replacement and five years for two seats in the upper circle for *Cats*. Hip replacement – private? No problem – straightaway. In fact, there's a special offer this month – buy two hips, get one free. Yes, you can bring your own anaesthetic, though we do have to charge corkage. [3]

This is all so much sharper than a generalized comment about the collapse of the National Health Service and the length of waiting lists.

The visual

Our society is dominated by the visual. The television shows pictures even when they are more or less meaningless – for example, library stills of children in classrooms as a backdrop to news of changes in GCSEs. Visual images also operate as a kind of shorthand, a code – a shot of the Eiffel Tower tells us that the setting must be France. How can an oral medium cope with the ever-present picture? The stand-up comic manages to do it by facial expression, gesture, movement, energy and by painting word-pictures.

Thomas Troeger offers the preacher a way of developing the visual element in the sermon. He suggests we tackle the question, 'How would you broadcast the Gospel to your people in a 30-second spot?' If we can produce a storyboard for a TV advertisement, we will have made a start on preaching visually. Troeger himself recounts his preparation for a wedding sermon. He began by producing a conventional sermon which is actually a very fine piece of communication. Here is a sample paragraph:

> Promise and covenant – for the rest of your lives remember these sacred words, these words rooted in the promises of God, these words that go deeper than feeling.
> Remember them in the night when a child cries.

Remember them when bitter speech has passed between you.
Remember them when your bodies fail from illness or age.[4]

This is visual speech: it is on its way to being concrete and specific. But in Troeger's opinion it does not take account of the visual orientation of today's listeners. The second version works hard on 'seeing', and is organized round sharply observed scenes, like video clips. Troeger imagines the couple having photographs taken each year on their wedding anniversary:

> Poorer. The word bursts like the flashcube on their friend's camera and highlights the stack of bills on the table beneath the phone, and the calendar marked with the doctor's appointments they cannot afford. A look leaps between them.
> 'We promised.'
> The camera flashes again.
> 'That will be a good one,' exclaims the friend.

> Next I picture the couple ten years later. Things are much better for them financially. The husband has a good job. The wife went back to school and has just taken an excellent position. The colonial love-seats by the fireplace have been re-covered in a quilted chintz. Each of the children has a ten-speed bicycle in the garage. But the husband and the wife have thrown acid words at each other.[5]

Troeger's second version uses all the devices of the television camera. It works with freeze-frames, with changes of angle and viewpoint, with close-ups and long shots.

PREPARATION AND PERFORMANCE

Professional speakers work hard. It is this which strikes me most forcibly when I watch them and listen to their patter. A few random thoughts thrown together and spoken off the cuff won't do. What can preachers learn?

73

Cut!

The comedian's material is ruthlessly pruned. Time constraints make for discipline: what doesn't work is cut. If you are likely to overrun, you shorten the script. If the producer says 4 minutes 25 seconds, that's what you get. There are few more exhilarating experiences than working with a director who exposes what is trite, trivial, meaningless, banal, boring or longwinded. The threat of the blue pencil concentrates the mind wonderfully.

Getting in, going on and getting out

The comedian and the after-dinner speaker work hard to hook the audience in the first few sentences. The politician makes sure that somewhere in the middle there's a memorable sentence, an image or saying that will do as a soundbite. Just remember how often the saying, 'Tough on crime, tough on the causes of crime', was recycled. Or from a different political party, Michael Heseltine's 'Left, left, left'. And every politician knows the importance of the out-line – that last phrase which will be remembered when the rest of the speech or interview is instantly forgotten. The professionals are aware of short concentration spans. They don't overestimate the interest of the audience. Since people will zap from channel to channel, it is vital to insert 'flashes' at regular intervals to recall a wandering audience. And if you don't strike oil quickly, stop boring.

Rehearse, rehearse, rehearse

Public speaking of any kind is a performance. Even though the sermon is a spiritual activity, it is still a performance. The professionals rehearse what they are going to say – even the most apparently spontaneous comedians like Ken Dodd and Frankie Howerd rehearsed the giggles, the nudges and the winks. Morecambe and Wise even rehearsed the mistakes. And, of course, they memorized the script. You can't imagine a comedian reading his or her material. The script is written with an ear to how it will sound when spoken: it aims for a conversational, almost artless, effect. But learning and rehearsing the content means that it can be

74

'brought off the page'. Paradoxically, it is the painstaking learning and practising of the material which communicates freedom, spontaneity and immediacy. Preachers who constantly have to consult their notes may in fact be nearer spontaneity than the comedian – but, rather unfairly, listeners are likely to conclude that they haven't really mastered their stuff.

Engage the listeners

Public speakers and stand-up comedians engage with their audience. They expect an audible response and would be crestfallen if they didn't get it. Their success depends on being keenly aware of what is going on out there, so feedback becomes all-important. Billy Connolly in full flood rides skilfully on the laughter. He sets up a kind of dialogue, whereby the audience, though its role is limited to laughter, is brought into the conversation at every point. Enormous effort is spent on building and maintaining rapport, and in this cause everything – gestures, looks, insults, rhetorical questions, strange accents, pregnant pauses, funny walks – may be thrown into the pot. Preachers need to have the same awareness of the effect they are having, and the same capacity to respond to it. This may smack of manipulation – but the methods do not have to be those of the demagogue. Black preachers, both African and American, seem to know instinctively how to 'work' a congregation and work with a congregation, in ways which respect their dignity.

Video a sermon from one of the Sunday television services, and any stand-up comedian who you find amusing. Compare the two performances. How much of the comedian's technique could be used by the preacher without trivializing or distorting the Gospel?

---

7 The shapely sermon

Sermons are cunningly crafted pieces of persuasion. Few preachers just let the words pop out and, if they do, the results are often incoherent and invariably too long. When the pews are hard, the congregation (if charitable and forbearing) spends a lot of its time turning the other cheek. Most preachers try to shape their sermons in advance so that they will achieve their aim.

If shape is related to purpose, then the structure and shape of a sermon is of paramount importance. It ought not to be a matter of accident or whim. In principle, preachers have a large menu from which to choose; in practice, they usually limit themselves to one or two preferred frameworks. Books on preaching list such diverse approaches as the expository, the developmental, the inductive, the deductive, the classificatory, the dialectical, the faceting, the narrative and the meditational. In his *Homiletical Handbook*, Donald Hamilton distinguishes between topical, textual and expository structures, and then goes on to look in detail at the keyword method, the analytical method, the problem-solving method, the comparative method, the syllogistic method, inductive patterns and narrative structures. When dealing with the textual method he identifies four subcategories – the implicational, the telescopic, the ladder and the illustrational.[1] There is an embarrassment of riches.

Recent work on the theory of preaching has emphasized that form is not just a handy receptacle into which one may pour the fine wine of the message. Like a receptacle, the form has a shape, and the liquid which is poured in will assume that shape. This probably does not matter much in the case of liquids (although some might balk at drinking an expensive wine out of a plastic bucket) – but in the case of sermons, the form will not leave the message unchanged. We have already noted how form creates expectations. The limerick rhyme-scheme encourages you to laugh;

'A panda went into a bar and ordered a pint and a sandwich …' is not a legal document; 'Doo-wah, doo-wah, diddy diddy doo' is unlikely to be part of a Requiem Mass. This suggests that there ought to be a suitable form for a particular message. It also raises the intriguing question of what happens when the preacher deliberately sets the message in a form not usually associated with sermons. And what is to be made of the fact that the Bible itself uses a variety of forms?

THREE POINTS AND A POEM

The commonest sermon-shape uses the three-point alliterative heading. This is a basic framework which, at its crudest, consists of point, illustration, application, multiplied by three. It is an eminently serviceable form, which some see reflected in Peter's sermon on the day of Pentecost – 'You crucified, God raised, we are witnesses' – only without the alliteration. It has been wittily characterized by Catherine Fox as 'the Barbour, Brogues and Bible school of preaching', because of its prevalence among a certain evangelical Oxbridge subculture. Its great merit is that it's easy to remember. From 40 years ago I can recall a sermon on 'Adam behind a tree, Christ on a tree, Zacchaeus up a tree'. It's all there – humanity's sin, atonement through Christ, the invitation to respond to the Gospel. The headings structure the message so firmly that most of us could have a stab at preaching the sermon from the headings alone.

Sometimes this shape exercises too strong a control. Ideally the three points ought to grow out of the passage and not be forced on to it. It is very easy to impose headings and categories which suit us, treating St Paul's subtleties as a tiresome distraction from what the congregation 'needs to hear'. Each point ought also to reflect the size and weight of the original. Reducing 14 verses to one heading, and then making a whole point out of two words, looks more like distortion than exposition. And it's always worth asking if the text really falls naturally into three sections.

Constant use of this structure raises other problems. When it is overdone it can result in sermons which are dull and predictable. Congregations get their weekly dose of Bible in the standard economy pack – something like the experience of watching a formula film, (*Rocky 1*, *Rocky 2*, *Rocky 3*, *Rocky 38*, etc. Isn't this where we came in?) The variety found in the Bible is flattened out.

And there is always the danger of going for pyrotechnics – nine alliterative points, with the headings getting longer and longer. Or coming up with strained headings: the flash-cards for one family service sermon (!) on Job were, 'Jehovah', 'Ombudsman' and 'Benediction'. I bet the six-year-olds enjoyed that.

GOING AND COMING

You finish reading a good book and turn the last page with a sigh of contentment. Just before you put it down, however, you turn back to the beginning and read the first few pages. Something has happened. It's happened to the characters in the story but it's also happened to you. You have changed. You see more clearly what is going on. Character traits, images and casual remarks which you missed first time around are now full of significance. A little while ago you set out from this point knowing more or less nothing; you have returned wiser and full of insight.

Some sermon structures reflect this experience – particularly that of faceting, in which the heart of the message is seen as a precious jewel which can be looked at from many different directions. Each angle of view adds something new. And at the end, the listeners have seen the central idea in a richer and deeper way.

One example of this structure came in a sermon on the encounter of the rich young ruler with Jesus (Mark 10.17–22). The preacher began with a naive and inadequate reading of the story which ended with the line, 'So it seems as if Jesus got his ethics wrong … [Long pause, puzzled scratch of the head.] But that won't do … Let's try again.' She then expounded the passage a second time and ended, 'So it seems as if Jesus got his theology wrong … But that won't do either … Let's try one more time.' The third reading produced a more faithful and satisfying explanation. This sermon 'moved', it did not stand in front of the story and pick out three distinct points to talk about, but moved out and then back, departed and returned.

I would include in this category most forms of artful and deliberate repetition, where the intention is to hark back and reactivate in the congregation's memory a phrase used earlier. A sermon on Jesus' meeting with the leper in Mark 1.40–45 ended each paragraph with the phrase, 'This is our God.' A famous sermon by Tony

Campolo was organized around the refrain, 'It's Friday ... but Sunday's coming!' Rowan Williams structured a short sermon on Peter's denial around four repetitions of the phrase, 'I do not know the man'. His last paragraph illustrates how the congregation can be led out and back, and can return to the theme statement with greater understanding as the preacher plays variations on knowing Christ:

> I shall never know him. There is always more than I can say or think ... I do not know him; all I have known is that in his silence and his death all men and women will find themselves free ... I do not need to know him, to master and categorise and theologise him ... I do not know the man; I want to be where he is.[2]

One further example is drawn from a sermon on Christmas by Mary Cotes called 'Standing in the stable'. The listeners are taken in imagination to the stable. They watch and hear Mary's pain. The section ends: '"How silently, how silently the wondrous gift is given." Or so the carol goes ... But do you still believe it, now that you are standing in the stable?' The second scene focuses on the moment of birth and ends: 'A new voice cuts the darkness. The baby is crying. The baby is crying his new life into us! "The little Lord Jesus no crying he makes." Or so the carol goes ... But do you still believe it, now that you are standing in the stable?' At the very end of the sermon, the phrase recurs:

> But perhaps also you came with me because you thought that God could only be found in some kind of comfortable fairy-tale world. Perhaps it was because you thought that you could not find God in your world, in your darkness, or in your struggle. Perhaps it was because you thought you could not find God in your own life, with all its relentless rhythm of calm and crying.
>
> Do you still believe it, now that you are standing in the stable?[3]

Such a structure can be deeply satisfying. The repetition has the same effect as a musical phrase underneath the main tune, holding the whole piece together. It's like reading a map before a journey, and then looking at it once the journey is over in order to match map with reality. You feel as if you've come home, but with a different perspective on the map and with a store of rich memories. It is also my impression that this structure makes for more memorable sermons. The main point is pressed deep into consciousness.

JOURNEYS

The structure of some sermons is more like a journey. People move when they are on a journey. Preacher and congregation do not spend their time contemplating a series of truths – as if they were standing in an art gallery looking at different pictures. Nor do they depart and return as if photographing the same subject from a number of different angles. They set out on a journey, looking towards their destination and leaving the point of departure behind.

This is not quite the same thing as movement, pure and simple. Sermons which consist of a number of unrelated moves are likely to be heard as disconnected and incoherent. 'The preacher just said the first thing that came into his head.' This is precisely the problem with verse-by-verse exposition. The phrase, 'And then he goes on to say', signals yet another paraphrase of a biblical verse. Far from qualifying as sound teaching, the sermon, like the famous definition of history, comes out as 'one damn thing after another'. Fourteen short comments on fourteen verses from St Paul are too many to hold in mind. And the sermon has no shape, plot, argument or development.

But journeys have a shape to them. They have a beginning, a middle and an end – or, as someone has said, 'a beginning, a muddle and an end.' The key is that something new happens: something is unfolded, or an apparently simple situation is complicated. It is not a matter of ambling along. Preachers do not invite their congregations to 20 minutes on the exercise bicycle – lots of effort but no progress. There has to be tension and resolution, mystery and revelation, plight and rescue. It would be good if there could even be some surprises.

If the sermon is a journey, it can climb a mountain, driving towards the summit, going higher and higher with each step and allowing better and better views, until it reaches the top and can look back over the trail or out across the landscape. The sermon can move upwards with mounting excitement or increasing conviction. If the sermon is a journey, it can thread its way through a labyrinth or forest. It can set out on a fine day, run into difficulties, encounter foes and vanquish them, endure ordeals, meet friends, bring them alongside and reach home safely.

In the last few years the study of sermon construction has concentrated on this kind of sermon. The most obvious example of the form is that of the story. However, to preach on a story in the Bible is not necessarily to set out on a journey. One common way of handling a story is to tell the whole story and then pick points out of it, thus turning it into the pictures-at-an-exhibition type of sermon. It is worth asking the question, 'What happens to a gospel story when it is freeze-framed and a number of static "points" distilled from it?' Usually movement and sequence tend to disappear. The storyteller's careful build up of suspense and surprise is flattened out. The 'point' of the story, which is likely to have been embedded in the narrative, has to be excavated and 'explained', as if you were telling someone the point of a joke.

Eugene Lowry has written extensively on the design of narrative sermons. In *How to Preach a Parable*, he sets out four basic structures for preaching Bible stories:

1 Running the story, in which the preacher weaves story and 'application' together, or disguises the application by incorporating it in the telling.

2 Alternating the story, in which a block of the story is followed by a block of commentary, to be followed by a further block of story.

3 Delaying the story, by starting the sermon with non-story material – a current concern or a problem to which the story is the answer – and bringing in the story when a twist or a surprise or a resolution is needed.

4 Suspending the story – a design characterized by beginning with the story, stopping when the story runs into trouble, and returning to the story once the trouble has been resolved.[4]

Four brief sentences will not do justice to Lowry's entertaining

81

analysis of these structures. In the course of the book, however, he makes some significant claims for sermons as journeys:

- It is possible to do greater justice to movement, sequence and surprise, and thus to reflect something of the shape of a biblical story.
- It may be easier to put the congregation in a position where they do not so much hear the truth as experience the truth – especially when the meaning comes packaged within the narrative and is fleshed out through dialogue, character and plot.
- A preacher who follows the twists and turns of the plot remains an explorer and an investigator, and is less likely to remain in command and turn into an explainer than the preacher who distils truth from a text.

What follows is an example of running the story (Lowry's first structure), in which the story and reflection are woven together. It might be a useful exercise to identify those phrases which 'tell the story' and those which add theological commentary on its significance.

By the river itself it was quieter. People fell silent. As if they sensed that something important could happen. Almost formed what you might call an orderly queue. Coming to John and being plunged into the water by him. And that was when Jesus came. Standing with the others, waiting his turn. Contained, silent. When he came to John, John was visibly shocked. Held him off. 'Not you. Never you. This is for the rabble, the sinners. You're not part of their world.' And Jesus put his hand on John's arm and said, 'Let it go. Right? This is where I'm meant to be.'

So I'm left with an image in the mind. A picture of Jesus coming up from the river, with the water streaming down his cheeks, streaking his face, like tears. And standing in the river, alongside the rest of the people, saints, sinners and solicitors. God doesn't cheat. He's down in the mess where we are. Immersed in our world. It's where he's meant to be. And over his head I saw the skies opened, and heard a voice speaking after long years of silence and saw the bird of heaven flying free.

I have chosen to spend time on the story because this is the most obvious form of the sermon as journey. But even Lowry's examples show that the journey sermon does not necessarily mean a story in the literal sense. What is important about the journey form is *movement*. At its simplest it consists of a setting, a complication and a resolution. For example, according to Lowry the journey form consists of the following sequence:

> Upsetting the equilibrium (Oops)
> Analysing the discrepancy (Ugh)
> Disclosing the clue to resolution (Aha)
> Experiencing the Gospel (Whee)
> Anticipating the consequences (Yeah).[5]

A sermon which consisted of a clear statement drawn from the text, followed by a problem, a question, an objection, or an expression of disbelief, followed by the text's answer to that complication, would have travelled on a journey.

PLAYING WITH FORMS

This chapter is about variety in sermon form. I hope it will lead to a greater willingness to experiment with the shape of the sermon. Clearly, a serious attempt to reproduce something of the form of the original passage is better than squeezing every literary type into the same framework. Is the passage a psalm (and if so, what kind of psalm?), a hymn, a meditation, an argument, a proverb, a conflict story, a blessing? Why then do we hear relatively little variety in sermons? The Bible contains taunt songs – but we seldom hear the preacher experiment with satire as a way of communicating truth. We might sometimes consider choosing a sermon form which would allow us to reproduce the mood of the original – or one which closely followed its movement. Again, paying attention to form encourages us to ask what the text is *doing*. Is it praising God,

complaining about his silence, telling me, exhorting me, or taunt-
ing and mocking evil? Can we ensure that the sermon tries to
achieve the same effect as the original? How often is the hymn to
Christ in Colossians 1 preached as a hymn rather than as an exercise in systematic theology? How do you preach a prayer without
destroying it as a prayer? Is there any way of preaching a Beatitude
so that it *conveys a blessing* instead of just describing those who are
blessed?

Here are some experiments with form. They invite others. The
first is the introduction to a sermon for St Barnabas' day.

> Dear Paul,
> I have just heard that you are in prison, so I write to send
> you my greetings. By what I hear, the law seems to be drag-
> ging its feet in your case; they tell me Felix wants to get out
> of taking a decision. Things are no better for me; I'm in
> custody too, but there is unlikely to be a delay. The author-
> ities want some martyrs to satisfy local unrest.
> I have been thinking again about our work together and
> about our dispute. From our first meeting, I knew that you
> were a precious addition to our growing fellowship of
> believers. There were many who thought otherwise –
> understandably, given your part in persecuting us. But
> because I was sure, I was glad to be able to encourage you,
> and to speak for you to the others in Jerusalem.
> But because I had done so for you, and because when we
> then went through so much together – wasn't it three towns
> we got thrown out of? – I was very hurt when you refused to
> take Mark with us. For I was also sure in the Spirit that
> Mark had great gifts.

The second example is from the beginning of a Christmas sermon
which sounds like a creation story.

> It is Christmas Eve in the year 2095.
> A tribe of desert nomads is sitting round the fire in an oasis.
> Grandad says to little Benjamin,
> 'Come on, it's time you went to bed.'
> 'But I won't be able to sleep, because that star is so bright.'

That night up in the sky was a star shining more brightly than
   all the others.
It was almost like a sun penetrating the blackness of the desert
   night.
'Why, Grandad, does that star shine so brightly tonight?'
Grandad thought for a moment and then said,
'Well a very long time ago before the world was made
God was all alone.
He was miserable.
He had no one to talk to,
No one to love and no one to be loved by.
So one day he said,
'I will make something fantastically beautiful.'

The third example is from the middle of a sermon on Psalm 22.
The preacher is somewhere around verses 12–21 and is trying to
echo the mood and imagery of the original while suggesting a
range of 'applications'.

My God, you have abandoned me. And you won't tell me
why.
I am at the stake. Baited by my enemies. They stand round
me in a circle. I am here – at bay.
The child taunted by bullies. The victim on whom they
practise their dark experiments.
The one who is jostled and mocked and cannot break out of
the ring.
They encircle me and taunt, jeer and deride. Their faces
distort, become animal like, bestial, demonic, the face of
the bull and the lion and the dog and the wild ox.

O God, I need you at my side. And you are on the outside
of the ring. Somewhere far away.

It is five in the morning and they file in and stand silently
round the bed. And the voices speak.
Such a plain child. An awkward lumbering creature.
You naughty, naughty girl. What a wicked thing to do.
You'll never make anything of yourself.
You must do better than that if you are to please Daddy.

If you behave like that Mummy won't love you any more.
They stand round me. O God, I need you at my side. And
you are on the outside of the ring. Somewhere far away.

The next example of imaginative use of form comes from near the
end of a sermon on Psalm 125, in which the preacher is trying to
balance the imagined experience of the psalmist with the imagined
experience of a twentieth-century Christian. Part 1 of the sermon
ends as follows:

> The service came to an end. Suddenly there was silence and
> then I heard a single voice, the priest, speaking from a long
> way away. Four words only. *Shalom* be on Israel. I can't trans-
> late *shalom* for you. We Jews are brought up on it. It's peace,
> wholeness, right relationships. Being at one with God and
> your wife and children, with your neighbours, your animals.
> It's health, prosperity, integrity, community, security. It's ...
> *shalom*. Peace be on Israel.
>
> I came back home with the family. Nothing much has
> changed. The land is still oppressed. Levi's son is still going
> to the dogs. And the new-fangled ways of the foreigners
> seem as fashionable as ever. But something has changed. I
> have seen something clearly. I know it to be true. The Lord
> surrounds his people as the mountains surround Jerusalem.
> In the end we cannot be shaken – not to the foundations.
> We can't be harmed ultimately; not deep inside, at the
> centre. He is our security. Nothing can get in between him
> and us. And one day he will shake the earth and make
> everything new and restore everything as it should be.
>
> So in that conviction I stumble from sabbath to sabbath.
> Not finding it easy but holding on, keeping faith with God
> as he keeps faith with me.

Five minutes later the preacher has reached the same point in Part
2, as he retells the parallel experience of Michael Robson, a
Geordie who works in South Shields:

> The service came to an end. Suddenly there was silence and
> then I heard a single voice, the minister, speaking from a

long way away. 'The peace of God, which passes all understanding, keep your hearts ...' Peace ... Wholeness, right relationships. Being at one with God and your wife and children, with your neighbours, your animals. It's health, prosperity, integrity, community, security.

I came back home with the family. Nothing much has changed. The papers and the television are as doom laden as ever; work is still difficult; the pressures on the Christian family seem as great. But something has changed. I have seen something clearly. I know it to be true. A mighty fortress is our God. The Lord surrounds his people as the cathedral shelters its worshippers. In the end we cannot be shaken – not to the foundations. We can't be harmed ultimately; not deep inside, at the centre. He is our security. Nothing can get in between him and us. And one day he will shake the earth and make everything new and restore everything as it should be.

So in that conviction I stumble from Sunday to Sunday. Not finding it easy but holding on, keeping faith with God as he keeps faith with me.

Go back over your last six sermons. How would you describe the basic shape of each one? Now choose *one* and attempt to incorporate the same message within at least two entirely different shapes. Does anything happen to the message as a result?

---

8 Faith, hope and clarity

> Hear how he clears the points o' faith
> Wi' rattlin' an' wi' thumpin'!
> Now meekly calm, now wild in wrath,
> He's stampin' an' he's jumpin'![1]

'Make it plain!' is the cry of the Black congregation urging their preacher to speak up, speak out and 'tell it like it is'. It has as much to do with passion as with clarity. But unfortunately passion can be the enemy of clarity: words tumble over each other as the preacher desperately tries to let out the fire that is burning within, and somewhere in the blaze coherence and intelligibility perish.

Maybe this doesn't matter too much if the message is full of fire. When the preacher is incandescent, the people will feel the heat even if they're not getting much light. (Even here, though, the choice should not be between *either* passion *or* clarity: it is possible to have both.) The real problem is when the sermon is neither passionate nor clear, when it's like a ball of wool after the cat's had it.

DANGLES AND FLIP-FLOPS

There are few experiences more maddening than listening to a speaker who indulges in what J. S. Kounin calls 'dangles and flip flops'.[2] By 'dangles' he means starting one activity and then leaving it abruptly to engage in another; 'flip flops' consist of ending an activity and then coming back to it unexpectedly. Although Kounin was writing about classrooms, his words apply equally well to sermons.

I want to speak this morning about the disciples, well, perhaps I ought to say the apostles, but, anyway, this passage calls them disciples even if we call them the apostles later. Well, not *us* exactly, but the tradition of the Church. It's not just something, you know, not just a term that we've made up. Anyway, the four disciples in John. Jesus called them. And you know, the Christian life is about discoveries. I know the other gospels have got twelve names – and incidentally some of the lists, you know, in the four gospels, don't exactly match – but we're going to look at the four mentioned in John chapter 1. Jesus called them in different ways. Each in a way suitable to their personality. Maybe you're thinking, 'Well, I'll sit back and relax now because I'm already a disciple, I've already been called.' Wrong. Always something new. Jesus always calls us on. Calls us on. The Christian life is about discoveries.

Three minutes of this and most of us have lost the will to live.

The excerpt above contains examples of both dangles and flip-flops. It would be useful to analyse the passage, identifying the main points the preacher is trying to make, setting on one side the unimportant asides, marking dangles and flip flops, and putting the key ideas into a logical order.

You might end up with something like this:

I want to speak this morning about the four disciples in John chapter 1.

- Church tradition calls them apostles.
- We often follow this tradition.
- We haven't just made it up.

- There are twelve names in the full list.
- The lists of disciples aren't precisely the same in all four gospels.

- Jesus *called* them.
- He called them in ways *suitable to their individual personalities*.

- But his call is not once and for all. He is always calling us on.
- So the Christian life is a life of constant discovery.

Being clear is not as easy as it seems. Perhaps a word from Einstein might depress us further. He was asked whether the theory of relativity was too difficult to explain to a school pupil, and replied that any scientist who cannot explain what he is doing to a reasonably intelligent 14-year-old is either incompetent or a charlatan. I'm not sure if Einstein was right in all cases, but we might take his comments as a challenge. To help us avoid being thought incompetent or charlatans, we must focus on the words we use, and on the way in which we arrange them.

WATCH YOUR LANGUAGE

The New Testament uses about 5,000 words. It is not 'high culture' – in fact, many modern translations try to smooth out some of its less polished passages. Where Paul says, 'I want you to know' several times in a row, a translation will ring the changes: 'I want you to appreciate … consider … recall … acknowledge'. But the original is seldom so sleek. Ordinary, honest, straightforward speech will do nicely for the preacher, except in those places where he or she wants a specific effect.

Below is a passage from a printed article. It would be difficult to preach. Simplify and recast the paragraph so that it can be spoken. If, in the process, the language becomes more vivid and memorable, so much the better.

Paul is both astonished and angered by the defection of the Galatians. To desert the liberty which Christ had brought, and to return to legalism is unthinkable. Nevertheless Paul gives no occasion for those who recognize their liberty in Christ to pervert that liberty into licentiousness.[3]

For what it's worth, here's one effort.

> I don't believe it!, says Paul. You are betraying Christ! How can you possibly do that? Christ gave you freedom. And now you want to go back into slavery. Because that's what it is – slavery. A life of keeping the rules, dotting i's and crossing t's. Have I done this, have I done that, have I avoided the other? Always worrying about keeping my nose clean. Will I be good enough to make the heavenly cut-off point? Look, Christ released you from all that. Set you free. Going back into it is a kind of betrayal.
> That's how Paul saw one group. The other lot were just as bad. Oh well, if Christ has set us free, we can live how we like. Oh no you can't, says Paul. It's not a licence for 24-hour sex. That is not what Christian freedom is about.

The revised version illustrates what happens when we turn a written text into the spoken word:

- The vocabulary moves down a level or two, and becomes colloquial.
- The new version is longer than the original.
- Sentences get shorter.
- There have to be more of them, since people cannot pick up meaning as quickly as from a printed page; nor can they go back to check what they've read.
- Direct speech pushes out third-person description
- If we 'hear' the second version in our heads, we realize how much of the meaning is carried by non linguistic elements like gesture, tone, facial expression, body language, emphasis.

Preaching is an oral activity. Being clear when you are speaking requires a different set of techniques from those which come into play when you are writing. Here are a few things to bear in mind (among dozens).

Avoid the language of Zion

The language of Zion includes Christian clichés: 'journeying mercies' ('I hope you don't crash'); 'I ministered to him' ('I made him a cup of tea'); 'It's good to fellowship with you' ('I've enjoyed our chat; let's do it again sometime); 'Let's move into a time of sharing' (Aaarrrgh!). But the advice also includes some technical terms, such as 'intercession' ('praying for other people'), or 'righteous' (often means no more than 'good, honest people who say their prayers and do their best', as in Luke 1.6 and 2.25. We don't have to be too Pauline.)

Don't be afraid of conversational patterns

Most of the country says 'you' and 'we'. One only says 'one' if one is a member of the royal family. Use the present tense ('God looks at us and says ...') and the active voice ('Someone told me this story', not, 'A story is told ...'). Shorten the sentences. Make use of exclamations and questions. Talk directly to the congregation as if you were having a conversation with them.

Use natural rhetoric

Many rhetorical devices are part of ordinary speech. For example, it is surprising how often *the rule of three* operates (and not just in jokes about Englishmen, Irishmen and Scotsmen): 'Jesus sits round the same table, eats off the same plates, cracks the same jokes ...'.

We often use *repetition* to hammer a point home. There is a reason for this. If a congregation cannot scan backwards and forwards across a text, then important points have to be underlined by a different method. Irate parents have used the technique for centuries: 'You are not going out tonight. Do you hear me? You are not going out tonight. Not tonight, not tomorrow night, not any night for the next week.'

Sometimes we can make use of artful *alliteration*: 'A ragged rabbi with a gleam in his eye'; 'Not cold, calculating, dispassionate, disapproving, the dispenser of good advice'.

THE CONGREGATION CROCODILE

These last examples remind us that clarity is more than just a matter of vocabulary; the way in which the words are arranged is also important.

I have found it helpful to compare preaching a sermon to taking a school party to a museum. The experienced teacher knows that it is easy to lose the odd child on the way, and therefore she organizes them into a two-by-two crocodile. Even if you don't actually lose any children, they may still find the visit confusing, and remember the pencil and rubber they bought in the shop at the end of the visit more clearly than the exhibits. Teachers put key strategies in place before they set out. What are the parallels for the preacher?

A ground plan

Separate parts of the sermon are like individual rooms. You need to make sure that you move through the rooms in a sensible order, and that each of the rooms is kept distinct and separate. A room inside another room, for example, can make for maximum confusion. Some museums have multiple exits from a central hall. We are grateful for the arrows which take us the right way round. As far as preaching is concerned, this analogy stresses the importance of your having a clear structure in your own head. You at least know the visiting order.

Some books advocate the old rule: 'First I tells 'em what I'm gonna say, then I tells 'em, then I tells 'em what I've told 'em.' I am less sure. Laying out the whole sermon at the beginning is high on clarity, but loses all surprise and suspense. It will be difficult to help a congregation feel the force of a problem if you have already told them your solution.

Whatever your views on this issue, however, the earlier example of dangles and flip-flops is in another league. Here there is no discernible structure or sequence. Rooms are nesting inside other rooms – and subjects overlap, interweave and are muddled up with extraneous and irrelevant material. (Fortunately only part of the example comes from a real sermon!) We need to watch for points which overlap, or for one point embedded in another, which needs to be taken out and told firmly to wait its turn in the queue.

Entering and leaving

British towns tell you when you enter them: a reassuring notice by the side of the road informs you that these are the outskirts of Hightown, that the town centre is ahead and that the ring road is off on the left. French towns are yet more obliging: the name of the town, helpfully crossed out, tells you that you are now leaving St Marie sur Plage. In the same way, sermons need signposts. To use a different metaphor, thresholds – that is the bits between rooms, the doorways – are dirty and dangerous. You lose people across thresholds: some stay behind; others rush ahead into rooms which are not on your itinerary. A congregation needs a clear signal that it is about to enter a new room.

Such signals are supplied through words. The equivalent of a large notice is two or three sentences which say more or less the same thing in different words. Such a bundle of sentences has enough weight to carry the new message and still to allow for the odd spot of daydreaming. But when we are speaking we seldom rely just on words. We also use non verbal means. We pause as if to take breath or stock, we look at people meaningfully, we change tone or volume, or shift our weight. One way or another, we will indicate that the shape of the sermon has altered: we are now setting off in a new direction.

It is even more vital to tell people when you are leaving the room. A proper exit involves firmly closing the door on the old room before opening the new one. Once again, we make use of a combination of verbal and non-verbal signals. Picking up the thought with which you began is the most obvious verbal way of ending a sequence. A certain finality of tone or slowing of pace are non-verbal signals which carry the same message. If we don't close the door properly, thoughts from the old room are liable to drift into the new one – or people will not even realize that they have entered a new room.

Orientation

Standing in a museum, somewhere between the Early Mesolithic artefacts and the coffee shop, you are relieved to find a map with an arrow indicating, 'You are here'. Framing statements do the same job for the sermon. They represent stopping places where the congregation can draw breath and glance back over the journey so far, before moving on to the next stage. They do not give away the surprise of what lies ahead – but they do help everyone see where they've got to.

Inside a room

Once inside a room a range of other strategies comes into play. Somewhere in the room is a key idea or a controlling concept. People need to grasp what that idea is; they need to make it their own. The next two chapters will explore some of the ways in which we try to achieve this. For the moment it will be sufficient to point up just four of the obvious techniques we use when trying to explain things.

EXAMPLES
Most people come to understand a concept either by hearing it described and then having it fleshed out with lots of examples or, conversely, by working out the meaning of a concept from a bundle of examples. Either way, examples play a key role in clarifying ideas.

NON EXAMPLES
Very often we come to understand the nature of something by means of a contrast – by hearing what it is *not*. 'When I say X I do not mean ...'

ANALOGIES
'It is like this' is a key element in explanation. We shall deal with the powerful tools of images and analogies in greater detail in the next section. However, it is my impression that reverse analogies ('It is not like this') do not work well, and are likely just to cause confusion.

PARAPHRASES
Paraphrasing is no more than saying the same thing in different words. However, paraphrases contribute to understanding in two

important ways: they give the congregation *time* (and time is the equivalent of scanning back across a written text); and for those who have not quite grasped what you are talking about, they offer a second or a third angle of view.

Too mechanical?

All this may sound rather cold and mechanical. Of course we ought to pay equal attention to the emotional weight and force of what we are trying to communicate. Someone said of the young Martin Luther King, 'I don't know what he's talking about but I sure like the way he's saying it.' However, while passion may communicate without clarity, there is no need to be passionately incoherent just to prove a point. Failure to observe some pretty basic rules is a major cause of muddled sermons. Congregations may not agree with us but they don't have to go home saying, 'What on earth was he going on about this morning?'

> This exercise too may seem rather mechanical, but I have found it extremely useful. Take an old sermon and list the main points you were trying to make. Now look for instances of the methods which I have mentioned in the last few pages, since the heading, 'The congregation crocodile'. How did you 'tell' the congregation that each point was starting, and how did you indicate that it was ending? Did you ever cause confusion by letting the end of one point drift into the start of the next? List all the 'signpost' words and phrases. Where did you draw breath and tell everyone 'this is where we've all got to so far'? How many examples, non examples and analogies did you use? Did you ever say the same thing in three different ways in order to let your listeners catch up?

9 The eggstain on the waistcoat

We've done our homework – our praying, reading and studying. We honestly believe that God has spoken to us through his word, and we have a reasonably clear idea about what we are to say. The beginning of an idea about a suitable shape is just forming in our mind. And now, just as we start to craft the sermon, the question of the right words becomes all-important: I've got good material but, oh woe and alack, it's the way I tell 'em that puts people to sleep.

It's very easy at this point to sermonize, to do what everyone expects sermons to do. Sermons preach at you – they exhort and harangue; they teach by instruction; they tell you what's what. This is the easy way to preach, and I can't blame anyone who wants to avoid the toil of working hard at a different kind of method, when the tried and tested one lies ready to hand.

But there is an alternative. A sermon might not *tell* the congregation so much as *show* them; it doesn't have to describe a situation when it can evoke it. Instead of hearing about a situation, a congregation could be helped to see it for themselves – it's the difference between listening to a report of an event or being present at it in person. Fred Craddock draws the moral for the preacher: 'The governing consideration in choosing words and phrases is that the goal is not to utter but to *evoke*, not to express anything about one's education, values, life or views of a text, but to *effect a hearing* of a text, of a message.'[1]

This is the way in which good dramatists and novelists work. Poor novels shove the message in your face. The good novelist isn't even looking at you when she writes. Her characters take on life independently of you. You eavesdrop on their story, you are the unseen listener at their conversations. You are not so much told that the mother is angry as see her white knuckles and pinched lips. You feel the grief of the daughter; she doesn't keep telling you, 'I'm really sad now'. And if there is a message, it comes through what you see and experience rather than what you are told directly. The Russian literary critic Gogol remarked, 'Show me the eggstain on a man's waistcoat and you will show me the man'.

Gogol's comment stresses the importance of the specific against the general, and the concrete against the abstract. It connects with our culture's natural preference for the visual – for pictures and snapshots. In a television-saturated world, it is not surprising that people are more deeply affected by what they *see* rather than by what they *hear*. This ought not to be a problem for the preacher whose sermons are taken from the Bible. Pictures came easily to the people of the biblical world. Somewhere along the way, propositions muscled in.

THE BARE BONES

The example which follows will give some idea of how bare a sermon can be when it is shorn of the specific detail, the concrete instance and the vivifying image. All the pictures and examples have been removed. What's left is thin – worthy, but a trifle wooden. The brackets mark the points at which the original sermon contained either a piece of imaginative reconstruction ('imagine the scene'), or a picture or analogy (an image), or an example (an instance), or a story (an illustration).

The Great Supper (Luke 14.15–24)

A man sitting at a meal with Jesus said, 'Blessed is the one who shall eat bread in the kingdom of God.' And Jesus tells the story of the great banquet (*Imaginative reconstruction*).

The story tells us first that Christianity is about enjoying yourself. Having a good time. It's about a God who is generous. It's about Jesus who was called a gluttonous man and a winebibber (*Image*). It's about heaven (*Image, Illustration*).

God is an includer, not an excluder (*Image*). He is generous, even extravagant. He gives at great cost to himself. For free. He wants other people's company. He includes people. He doesn't shut them out (*Illustration*).

God says, 'I want my house to be full' (*Imaginative reconstruction*). The picture given here of life in the kingdom is one of acceptance (*Image*), of satisfaction (*Image*) and joy. All from the hand of this generous and extravagant God.

You wouldn't dream of turning down an invitation to this kingdom, would you?

They do. The oxen, the field, the new wife (*Imaginative reconstruction, Image*). All good things, but they get in the way. They are half reasons and half excuses (*Instances*).

I understand those reasons. I feel the force of the excuses. And yet, the invitation to the feast comes to us – in obvious and not so obvious ways (*Instances*). Jesus says, 'Enter into the life I offer you. Don't miss the feast' (*Instances*). I don't know in what form the invitation comes. But don't turn it down. Don't miss the party.

The story has a bitter-sweet ending. The house is full. And the guests are nothing special (*Imaginative reconstruction*). God's not choosy. He takes us as we are.

But the same generous God who invites us allows us to refuse the invitation. He respects our wishes. Quite a compliment really (*Illustration*). The life of the kingdom is offered. If we turn it down we don't get it. So the householder's last words are, 'None of those who were invited will taste my banquet'. A bare fact.

Don't miss the party.

IMAGINATIVE RECONSTRUCTION

Imaginative reconstruction is an attempt to flesh out the scene. It involves seeing and hearing what is going on, and helping the listeners to be present at the occasion. This requires an exercise of imagination – but it ought to be imagination disciplined by the passage and by what may reasonably be inferred from it. Many biblical passages are short on detail. The preacher draws upon various things: the clues given in the text, such background material as can be found from the commentaries and dictionaries, a common humanity, and his or her own imaginative capacity for living in the scene. The demand is not much different when the scene is a non-biblical one: the situation must still be brought alive in a way which is at least in harmony with its basic framework.

Here is an example of this kind of disciplined imagination at work. It comes from a Christmas sermon in which the congregation has been taken to the stable:

> Then, suddenly, there is a cry to break into us, a scream to break the rhythm and to hang, haunting the darkness. Then quiet. This time a deep quiet. A quiet of relief and exhaustion. We wait, silently, sharing the quiet, not daring to punctuate it even by our breathing ... And then the sound we have been waiting for ... Listen. A new voice cuts the darkness. The baby is crying. The baby is crying his new life to us![2]

The imaginative reconstruction ought to grow out of the text and not go wildly beyond it unless as part of a deliberate strategy. What is your instant assessment of the following excerpt from a sermon by A. J. Gossip?

> 'What are you going to be?' the boys would say as they trooped home from school, to him among the rest. And he would answer, 'Oh I must go to the workshop'. And he did, while others went to college and became successful men. In course of time they would come home for a holiday to the old village ... and folk would tell each other how well they had done ... While Jesus was the carpenter whom they ordered about.

I'm uncomfortable with this: we simply don't know that much about the home life of Jesus.

Despite my cautiousness, I still want to leave open the possibility that, at times, the reconstruction might be part of a deliberate strategy. Anachronisms often work in this way. Here is the opening to the sermon outlined above, on the Great Supper. Some of it can be reasonably inferred from the text, but this is interwoven with material drawn from a modern setting.

A man reclined at a meal with Jesus. And stretching comfortably after his third glass of wine said, 'This is a bit like heaven. Blessed is the one who shall eat bread in the kingdom of God.'

And Jesus said, 'Make sure you answer the invitation. Don't miss the party. Think on and look sharp.' (I bet that ruined his Black Forest gâteau.)

This process is taken still further later on in the sermon:

The story has a bitter-sweet ending. The house is full. And the guests are nothing special ... The poor, the maimed, the blind, the lame. The deadbeats, the tramps, junkies, hookers, layabouts, dossers and toe-rags, car thieves, a couple of Sunderland supporters, the cast of *Neighbours*, three traffic wardens and a rural dean. People like us. God's not choosy. He takes us as we are.

IMAGES

Images consist of pictures, analogies and metaphors. They are vivid and memorable, and represent a key element in preaching because they have the power to change the way people see the world. They are not padding for an undernourished homily, nor are they just a matter of peppering the discourse with picturesque speech in the style of a *Reader's Digest* special feature. Images are like burrs which stick on our clothes: we can't easily shake them off. Walter Brueggemann sees images as being at the heart of the transformation process: 'People in fact change by the offer of new models, images and pictures of how the pieces of life fit together – models, images and pictures that characteristically have the particularity of narrative to carry them.'[3]

In everyday life people will often think in pictures. 'Let me draw you a diagram. Look, here's your U-bend.' And ordinary conversation is stuffed full of powerful images, many of them robust, coarse, vigorous and sinewy. Take for example:

- 'Why buy a book when you can use the library?' (said by a man asked why he didn't settle down and marry);

- 'The light's are on but there's no one at home.'
- 'One sandwich short of a picnic.'
- 'All fur overcoat and nae knickers' (much, much stronger than 'She's a hypocrite').

In the same vein Jesus used picture language. 'Don't blow your trumpet before men', he said (Matt. 6.2). The Good News Bible, worried by the strong image, has served up a careful and anaemic paraphrase: 'When you give something to a needy person do not make a big show of it.' Oh dear!

Strong pictures and vivid images have the power to go on working after the speaker has finished. We remember the damning phrase, 'It was rather like being savaged by a dead sheep,' even when we have forgotten which MP said it about which of his political opponents.

Here is an example of an image which presents Christ as one who summons us to take risks but knows our frailty: 'He doesn't stand on the other side of an impossibly high wall and shout, "Follow me" over barbed wire and broken glass.' And here, from a sermon on 'God's motley carnival', is an image of the Church which offers the congregation a new way of seeing themselves in the world:

God's motley crowd – all with different functions, different personalities, differently dressed and so on, but all together in one purpose. In the carnival you have got jugglers, clowns, the strong man, musicians, dancers, acrobats, fire-eaters, magicians, the person who spins plates and the person who sells hot-dogs. And the carnival brings joy, vitality, energy, life – and it moves on like the pilgrim people of God.

INSTANCES

Instances are a third way in which we can flesh out the message. They are distinct from images in that, whereas images are invitations to see something *as if it were like* something else, instances consist of *real examples* of a general idea. We should not be surprised at the vital role they play in preaching. It is God's style to incarnate ideas, and if the Word became specific and individual, a real human being in a particular place at a definite point in history, then our general statements may as well follow suit.

Instances are powerful because they show you what it might be like to believe this truth, follow this exhortation, or work out this vision in daily life. John Robinson described the Sermon on the Mount as a set of instances – examples of 'the sort of demands love might make upon you at any time'. We are used to sermons which offer us a metaphor or an exhortation ('So let us all, this Lent, follow Jesus into the wilderness') – but frequently they leave the listener asking, 'Please tell me plainly what it might *mean* for me to "follow Jesus into the wilderness this Lent?"'

I offer two examples, the first from a wedding sermon: 'Of course, Alex and Alison are going to experience those little tensions which married life brings'. This is a general comment and needs to be earthed. What happens when the preacher instantiates the idea?

> It won't be long before she is screaming inside. 'He always leaves the top off the toothpaste and never puts the wheelie bin out!' Meanwhile he's muttering to himself, 'She always gets marmalade on the newspaper *and* finishes the quick crossword before I've seen it!'

The second example comes from part of an exposition of Colossians 3.13, and is on the phrase 'showing forbearance': 'Paul tells us to show forbearance – in other words, to put up with it'. This is too general a comment to bite; it's not much more than a paraphrase. Contrast it with this:

> There's this man in the church and he sniffs. He sniffs … all the time, he never stops sniffing … Great house-shaking, earth-moving sniffs. Sniffs that start at the toes and move up right to the top of the head. It's driving me mad! Then Paul's words come back to haunt me. 'Forbear. Put up with it. What makes you so perfect?'

The particular instance offered by the preacher is likely to fit very few people exactly – but it's my impression that a specific instance, even if it does not exactly fit my situation, is still much more helpful to me than the general comment or principle. Exhortations for me to apply the truth for myself do not work; seeing the general principle being applied to others actually helps me see to see what it might mean for me.

Here is a sequence of instances taken from the Great Supper sermon. They try to specify ways in which someone might 'answer the invitation to the banquet' – a metaphor which needs to be unpacked somehow.

Christ says 'Enter into the life which I offer you. Don't miss the party. What might that mean?

Perhaps I ought to join those confirmation classes. Or at least find out more.

I need to sort out ten minutes a day to pray. My life's a mess.

I could get stuck into the life of the church. I'm a passenger.

My Christian profession is a sham. I'm not what I seem to be. I've got to talk to someone fast.

We don't pray together as a couple. I don't think we're helping the children grow up as Christians. Why can't I talk to my wife or husband about it?

I just need to know how I can become a Christian.

You are preaching on Jesus washing the disciples' feet, and have just said something like, 'So we see that we should be prepared to serve one another'. What slices of real life (i.e. instances) flesh out this idea?

Later in the sermon you speak about the transitory nature of life – that sense that nothing lasts, everything decays. You have even launched into hymnody and Shakespeare ('Time like an ever-flowing stream bears all its sons away ...'; 'Life's but a walking shadow ...', etc.). Suddenly the thought strikes you that you need some instances to keep your language in touch with the ground. Try to think of three examples.

Two instances I've used for the second idea are:

- 'Growing out of your clothes through childhood' (or 'Being unable to get into your wedding suit');
- 'The way rust eventually eats away at the bodywork of the new car'.

10 A funny thing happened to me ...

Illustrations are the windows of the sermon; they let the light in and are often the part most people remember. They also need careful handling: there is nothing quite like a wayward illustration to blow a sermon out of the water. Richard Lischer observes: 'Illustrations often assume a life of their own and neither the preacher nor the congregation can remember what they were illustrations *of*.'[1]

ILLUSTRATIONS AS LITTLE STORIES

I am using the term 'illustration' to mean little stories – they are like instances or images in some respects, but they have grown up into narrative. The instance or the image tend to be one-liners or static snapshots. Illustrations are longer; they have a beginning to set the scene, a middle to develop or complicate the plot, and an ending to resolve it.

> In this chapter we shall look at the power of illustrations for good and ill. At the outset it would be useful if you could write out two illustrations to serve as reference material for some of the points I shall be making. You can then check my assertions against these examples.

• First, think of a story which will illustrate the idea of forgiveness.

- And second, think of a story which expresses the experience of awe and wonder, that strange mixture of terror and fascination, which some see as the heart of religion.

WHY DO PREACHERS USE ILLUSTRATIONS?

Illustrations perform at least five functions, some of which may seem rather strange.

1 Engaging attention

Stories are interesting. Everyone knows that a well-placed tale will revive the concentration of a flagging congregation. 'Begin with a story' seems to be received wisdom. The story may be a personal anecdote, a topical reference (in other words, an allusion to a story which everyone already knows) or a fully fledged narrative lasting several minutes and 'carrying' a theological message. Here, above all, it is vital that the story be stitched tightly into the body of the sermon.

2 Capturing goodwill

This may seem an unworthy use of an illustration, but the Romans recognized the importance of what they called *captatio benevolentiae*, or getting the audience on your side. Rewarding the congregation with an illustration allows them to relax a little before attempting the steep climb to the summit which you have planned. It's the equivalent of a short sit-down and a Kit Kat. Coming at the beginning of the sermon, the illustration says indirectly what I once heard an American preacher say directly: 'This ain't gonna be so bad. Or so long ... I hope.' Maybe that's why so many sermons begin with The Joke. Unfortunately very often the joke has little or nothing to do with what follows. That doesn't stop it hanging around for the next 20 minutes and beyond, muttering in the background.

3 Sending out important signals

Illustrations speak volumes about the preacher, about his or her message and about the congregation – because illustrations can never be value-free or neutral. They can't avoid referring to a particular culture and suggesting a particular attitude towards that culture. One important *function* of an illustration, even though this may not be its prime *purpose*, lies in its capacity to win acceptance for the preacher and, indirectly, for the message. For example, an illustration drawn from the world of football may lead the listener to think, 'This preacher really knows my world'. A reference to bringing up children may produce the reaction, 'This message really matches my life experience'. At the same time, the illustration is sending an implied message about the culture of the congregation ('Oh, so watching *Blind Date* isn't moronic'; 'Listening to Classic FM is all right'). Illustrations are never value-free.

The reverse is also true – and herein lies one of the dangers of illustrations. What is the effect of a sermon which draw all its illustrations from the eighteenth century? Or disparages the football-crazy culture of the area? Or appears to be ignorant of the latest pop group or film? Or stereotypes women? Or assumes a world where you can meet your accountant in the jacuzzi? Or supposes that children will possess dressing gowns? Every one of those examples has caused problems to someone of my acquaintance.

Since illustrations are double-edged, it will help if we comb through our illustrations and note all the subcultures to which they refer. Then we need to examine them. Are they drawn mainly from one or two areas of life? Are certain subcultures always seen positively or negatively? Are there damaging stereotypes? Or political, class, gender or racial prejudices? Go back to the two illustrations you wrote at the start of this chapter and examine them critically in the light of these questions.

I hope that the exercise was a useful one. It may have pointed up problem areas in your preaching. Unfortunately, part of the power of the illustration lies precisely in its particularity. This means that it will always run the risk of presenting the particular as the norm – it will, in other words, always tend towards stereotyping its main characters. You cannot use a story about care for a disabled person without running the risk of implying that all disabled people are helpless. You may have used an illustration which speaks about your grandmother's beautiful embroidery, intending that it should illustrate God's providence (believe me, it's possible!). Alas, you find out at the door that it has exasperated those listeners who have spent a lifetime trying to change the image of the domesticated woman. All we can do is be aware of what we are doing, be as sensitive as possible and go for variety and diversity in our illustrations.

Behind this advice lies the need to know the cultures of the congregation. There is a famous illustration taken from Helen Waddell's novel about Abelard. Abelard and Heloise are walking in a wood when they see a tree which has been chopped down. Abelard points out the rings which are seen in cross section, and observes that those rings run all the way through the trunk. 'We only see them here, at the point where the tree has been cut. God's love is like that. It runs from eternity to eternity but we see it in the cross section which is the death of Christ.' It's a powerful illustration but it carries overtones which may not be helpful for some congregations. 'Here is our minister talking about people with strange names who lived a long time ago. Who's Helen Waddell? Is she from the twelfth century? Abelard ... what kind of a name is that?' We can perhaps understand why one preacher decided to make the same point by using an illustration of a stick of rock. 'When you break a stick of rock it says "With love from Bridlington" all the way through.'

4   Clarifying a difficult concept

The obvious purpose of the illustration is to clarify a difficult idea or concept – and you may wonder why I have taken so long to get to this point. Illustrations express likeness – that is, in some way every illustration has the *same shape* as that which it is designed to illustrate. 'It is like this', is a powerful explanatory tool. But, equally and obviously, illustrations are also *different* from what they illustrate: they work precisely by being like X but not exactly like X. (If they were exactly like X they would *be* X and not much good as an illustration!) We select an illustration because we see some way in which it is similar to the idea we wish to clarify. We discern some common ground, while being aware that there isn't total correspondence.

So far so good: but the trouble comes with the leftovers. It is the part of the illustration which is *not* common ground that can wreak havoc on a sermon. Some of the elements are a necessary part of the story; some are minor details which the listeners will hardly notice. But the sermon goes awry when elements in the story set up dissonance with the idea the story is intended to illuminate. Then the congregation are likely to be troubled, incredulous, confused, exasperated or even sickened. I need to illustrate this point and will do so in a moment – but first, I want to link it with the final function of illustrations.

5 *Communicating emotional weight*

Illustrations come laden with freight. Every story carries its own emotion. Characters will be nice or nasty, wise or foolish, cruel or compassionate, held up as ideals or as dreadful warnings. The ending will be sad or funny, moving or inspirational. But the emotions of the illustration will tend to 'leak' into the point you are making. Illustrations are seldom watertight: they almost always leak. Or if you prefer, illustrations are like the filters on stage lights in a theatre, which colour the concept they illustrate. The preacher encourages the congregation to listen to the story, and then to move back into the theme of the sermon. But something of the story lingers on.

In the case of well chosen illustrations, this is all to the good. It gives the message emotional power; it is one of the ways in which the heart is warmed and the eyes opened. But a badly chosen illustration will sabotage what follows.

WHEN ILLUSTRATIONS DON'T WORK

These five functions of illustrations can help us see why some illustrations go wrong.

1 Engaging the attention

Illustrations fail to engage attention:

- When they are so dull or unremarkable that the listeners are not gripped by them.
- When they introduce irrelevant issues and concerns (which hook the listeners and encourage them to daydream).

2 Capturing goodwill

Illustrations fail to capture goodwill:

- When they constantly refer to the preacher, depicting him or her as hero, or as a victim; or inflicting a never-ending string of anecdotes about his or her family, pets, hobbies, early life, grandmother.
- When they cross the line between genuine personal testimony and exhibitionism. Sometimes a preacher exposes the congregation to information about his or her private life which is too embarrassing or too emotionally raw for them to handle. Half want to flee the building; the other half want to give the preacher therapy.

3 Sending the right signals

Illustrations fail to send the right cultural signals:

- When they appear to criticize the listeners' world from a superior position.
- When they are remote from, or place the preacher in a world which is alien to, the congregation's world.
- When a number of illustrations all come from the same area of experience (e.g. all from football or opera, or all about the preacher's new baby).

4   Clarifying ideas

Illustrations fail to clarify ideas:

- When they are more complicated than the idea they are intended to simplify.
- When they illustrate a slightly, or even an entirely, different idea.
- When the illustration begins by illustrating one idea, and then drifts off the point, finally illustrating a different idea.

5   Communicating the right emotional weight

Illustrations fail to communicate the right emotional weight:

- When they are trite, unrealistic, mawkish, sentimental or dishonest.
- When their 'emotional charge' is disconcerting in a way not designed by the preacher – for example, the illustration may be too powerful or carry the wrong associations. It may be mechanical or impersonal, where the idea requires something warm and personal – or funny where the idea is a solemn one.

Go back to the two illustrations which you wrote down at the beginning of the chapter. Assess their effectiveness in the light of the five functions (engaging attention, capturing goodwill, sending the right signals, clarifying ideas, communicating the right emotional weight). Do they fail on any of the criteria listed above?

SOME EXAMPLES

I end this chapter with one or two illustrations which I have heard recently, and yet which seem to have been in the system for years, if not centuries. They represent the kind of illustration which John Ortberg has wittily described as coming 'at the bottom of the homiletical food chain'. Their persistence is a mystery.

The first is a Christmas story. A young man and a young woman are deeply in love. He has an expensive watch, she has beautiful long hair. By a credible twist of fate, he has no chain for the watch and she has no brush and comb for her hair. On Christmas Eve he goes out and sells his watch in order to buy her a brush and comb, while she ... yes, she gets her hair cut off and sells it in order to buy him a chain.

The story is intended to illustrate sacrificial love. And it does. Unfortunately, the situation strikes the listener as sickly and artificial. What century are these people living in? (Watch and chain?) Their arrangements for sorting out Christmas presents don't correspond to any household I know of. The end of the story is likely to evoke laughter in a society brought up on *Private Eye* and *Men Behaving Badly*. And so on ...

The second story concerns a bus driver taking a coachload of daytrippers for a drive in the country. By chance he drives through the very village where his own child lives. As he rounds the bend his child steps out in front of the coach. The driver has a split second to decide whether to jam on the brakes and risk an accident which may kill all his 42 passengers, or drive over his child. You will not believe the ending.

This story has all the marks of a contrived piece of fiction. It is intended to parallel the love of God who did not spare his Son but sent him to die for humanity. As it stands it is a crude device which leaves the congregation asking what kind of a calculating robot is this father, and what kind of a bus driver. Leaving aside the coincidences which beggar belief, we still want to know if he might possibly have jammed on the brakes, swerved, taken a chance – and how he lived with himself and his wife afterwards. And what does it imply about God as a father?

Both stories illustrate what happens when functions 1, 3 and 5 go wrong. I have similar problems with the story of the world-famous pianist who found a child on the platform banging on the piano just before a concert in the Carnegie Hall. Apparently he crept up behind the child and improvised wonderful variations on a theme of *Chopsticks*. I'm afraid I don't believe it. (How did the steward who let the kid on to the platform keep his job?) And then there's the story of the judge who sits in judgement on his own son, fines him the maximum penalty and then pays it himself. How can we take this seriously? (Shouldn't he have declared an interest?)

It will be more positive to end with an illustration which works (I think). It is taken from a sermon by John Taylor, called *In Him was Life*, and is used 'as an instance of the effect of the really alive upon the half-dead'.

> A few years ago *The Listener* carried the script of a radio talk by an American woman who has pioneered ameliorative work among the very old. She described a typical institution she had visited.
>
> They were all sitting half-dead in their wheelchairs, mostly paralysed and just existing, they didn't live. They watched some television, but if you had asked them what they had watched they probably would not have been able to tell you. We brought in a young woman who was a dancer and we told her to play beautiful, old-fashioned music. She brought in Tchaikovsky records and so on, and started to dance among these old people, all in their wheelchairs, which had been set in a circle. In no time the old people began to move. One old man stared at his hand and said, 'Oh, my God, I haven't moved this hand in ten years.' And the 104-year-old, in a thick German accent, said, 'That reminds me of when I danced for the Tsar of Russia.'[2]

PART FOUR

Respecting the Listeners

11 Six feet above contradiction?

Preaching can be a wonderful ego trip. Even in a modern church dedicated to St Habitat, the pulpit is likely to be raised a foot or two. In a traditional building, you might be as much as six feet above ground level, standing while the congregation sit, and, despite the odd badly placed pillar, easily the most visible thing for 50 yards, except for the East window. Nervous? Don't you believe it! It's every extravert's dream come true.

Then again, in some way you have been recognized by the Church – as priest, minister, reader or local preacher. You are a person in authority. You may wear robes. You stand in the tradition of Luther, Wesley and Spurgeon. Nor do you speak in your own name: your opening prayer has probably made that clear. Preachers bring to the congregation nothing less than 'the word of God'. Moreover, this particular sermon is the fruit of much study and research. You and a handful of internationally famous academics, aided extraterrestrially by the Great Saints of the Church, have sorted out a timely word to which these people are now required to give attention without interruption. The sound of your own voice is more musical than that of the nightingale. And there is a kind of superiority that consists in being ever so humble and asking for the prayers of the people as you, all unworthily, shoulder the burden (but the very important burden) of bringing the word of God down from Sinai. Is there any situation quite like this? No wonder it's hard to keep your feet on the ground.

I hope this picture is a caricature. Few preachers in their right minds will think in this way. Nevertheless, the situation in which the sermon is delivered naturally feeds the preacher's sense of superiority. However broken and meek the preacher, however conscious of his or her shortcomings and limitations, the fact remains that he or she will be the focus of attention at a key point in the service – and this fact will subtly affect the way in which the situation is perceived.

At a Roman triumph, one man was given the duty of standing in the chariot behind the all-conquering general. His job was to intone into the victor's ear, 'Remember thou art but a mortal'. We need someone behind us to whisper, 'The Lord opened the mouth of the ass', and, 'Most of them are counting the panes of glass in the East window'.

It is perilously easy to patronize the congregation. They are there to be fed. They are the hungry sheep looking up with mouths open. It is a one-way process: you give, they receive.

This seems to be the view of preacher and congregation held by John Calvin:

> For this end and purpose he [God] has appointed shep-herds in his church which have the office and charge of teaching ... We see he deals with us after our weakness and chews our morsels for us that we might digest them the better, in that he feeds us like little children.[1]

Unfortunately, this view of the congregation as little children in highchairs, needing their food cut up (and chewed) for them, has had the effect over the years of giving the Scriptures to a preaching class. In the process it has probably done preachers' humility no good, and may have systematically deskilled congregations until no one dares utter a thought without checking it with the experts.

David Norrington has said as much in a book which is a sustained attack on the sermon as the Church presently understands it.[2] He argues that, while in theory the regular sermon need not inhibit participation, in practice it encourages dependence on the preacher. Ironically, the better the preacher, the more likely it is that the congregation will come to expect to be fed in this one-sided way. Congregations which 'are greatly blessed in their minister' may be missing out on possibilities of mutual instruction and support. The sermon encourages a passive attitude. The so-called teaching sermon (an extended discourse of 20–30 minutes of biblical exposition) is a notoriously ineffective method of teaching.

Because the method of communication is one way, it allows little interaction, questioning, disagreement or consideration of alternatives. At its worst, the system feeds the myth of the omnicompetent clergy, and the personality cult of the Big Name to which some Christian traditions seem especially prone. Instead of growing into mature Christian faith, congregations are kept in a condition of learned dependence.

These are serious charges and ought not to be dismissed out of hand. Unfortunately I cannot address them adequately here. But a book such as this one would hardly be written by someone who accepted Norrington's thesis in its entirety. For example, I would argue that young Christians are nourished in their new faith by a clear presentation of Christian truth. I also think that there are occasions in most people's lives when they need to be 'told' – and the kind pastor will tell them, not invite them into a discussion. Nevertheless, Norrington has a point. Given that the regular sermon will and probably should continue, how can we ensure that it does not produce the damaging effects which Norrington cites? Can congregations work more closely with preachers, and can sermons encourage interaction rather than passivity and dependence?

THE POWER OF THE PEOPLE

We should note first, though, that congregations are not without power. Any preacher will tell you that he or she can see a tell-tale movement of the head towards a neighbour, or the surreptitious glance at a wristwatch, from 60 feet away. We are acutely conscious of people's eyes and body language, and we react automatically in response. The influence of the congregation on the preacher is considerable – and is not always benign. We know, for example, that congregations can affect what counts as the normal length of the sermon. A friend of mine went as a guest preacher to a neighbouring church during an interregnum. He was told kindly but firmly, 'We don't have anything more than four minutes here'. One wonders how long it had taken the congregation to lick the previous minister into shape.

Congregations play a significant part in perpetuating other aspects of the subculture. Congregation and preacher together can collude in hearing and preaching sermons that everyone wants. An American minister told me that he was required by his denomination to finish every sermon with an evangelistic appeal, even though he knew that everyone in the congregation had been a paid-up member of the denomination for many years. The effect of this weekly requirement on his preaching ministry was disastrous. The natural logic of the sermon was regularly disrupted by an artificially imposed constraint.

Communities have their own strategies for understanding texts. They will correct interpretations and bring subtle pressures to bear on any which do not conform. Congregations have ways of letting the preacher know what is and is not acceptable in the pulpit, with comments such as: 'We don't want any more of that drama in the sermon'; 'We could do with less politics'; 'We don't like the OHP, it reminds us of school'. Preaching is partly determined by the question, 'What will the customers make of this?'

The effect of this question on the content and theology of the sermon has been investigated in depth by Marsha Witten.[3] She analysed 47 sermons, preached in Presbyterian and Southern Baptist churches in the USA, on the parable of the Prodigal Son. In the course of this analysis she noticed the ways in which preachers package traditional doctrine so as to make it conform to the sensibilities of people living in contemporary American culture. They assert 'traditional concepts of sin and its consequences, but with the rhetorical demeanor of a softened, genteel, and inoffensive style of speech called civility.'[4] They also project sin away from the congregation. For example, they deflect sin on to outsiders (by using illustrations involving children, adolescents, drug addicts, alcoholics, gamblers or prostitutes), or mitigate the sins of insiders (by describing the sins as possession of a nasty personality, or the wrongdoer as a lost child wandering from the path), or treat them tolerantly like a therapist (by describing sinful behaviour in value-free terms and empathizing with the hurts caused to the self as it pursues its misguided course).

The whole study is a painful warning about what happens when we reframe theology under social pressure. Here are preachers who are adjusting the content of the message to the expectations of their congregations. Congregations may be passive in some contexts; they are irresistibly powerful in others.

CO-OPERATIVE MOVEMENTS

The discussion so far may seem to be unnecessarily adversarial. I seem to be saying that preachers patronize and deskill congregations, and that congregations, since they shape preachers in their own likeness, need to be wooed and cosseted. Is it possible for preacher and congregation to work together? I offer some tentative suggestions.

1   The Bible belongs to all

Preachers need to operate with a clear understanding in their own minds that the congregation owns the Scriptures. God gave the Scriptures to the Church – in other words, to the whole people of God. Ordination or licensing can lead to a mind-set which unconsciously assumes that the Scriptures belong to the preaching class. After all, we may think, we have spent a long time studying and preparing for this moment. Out of all that perspiration and reflection we shall graciously vouchsafe to throw a crumb in the direction of the people. The truth is quite different. It is the Church which recognizes the preacher. It is the congregation which graciously authorizes us to speak from the Scriptures on this occasion. And the Scriptures are as much their possession as ours. This truth is emphasized in different ways in different denominations. In Anglicanism, for example, the liturgy is saturated with Scripture and the public reading of Scripture is given a very high profile.

2   The preacher is dispensable

Preachers also need to recognize that the congregation is able to come to maturity in Christ, and put the word of God into practice, without their help. Martyn Lloyd Jones said that he had heard better discussions on the theology of the Epistle to the Romans in the Welsh valleys than among his sophisticated congregation at Westminster Chapel. The miners, though lacking formal theological training, were used to debating theology, the issues were important to them and they assumed that each had something important to contribute. Similarly, Carlos Mesters has charted the astonishing changes which resulted when Christians in the base communities of Brazil took the Bible as their book, and reflected on its message in the context of the problems of their own lives.[5] As an illustration of the confidence brought about by this new orientation, he cites an incident which took place in one of the meetings:

> 'Sister I'm not going to say anything because I don't understand these things. I'm just going to listen and learn.' That was Dona Getulina's reply when Sister Vicentina asked her if she could give an opinion on the Bible passage read in the meeting. Another woman, Dona Florentina, did not give the Sister time to reply, but cut in: 'Dona Getulina, you mustn't say you don't know anything. You have the Holy Spirit. He speaks to you and you pass on his message to us.'[6]

This kind of freedom brings its own problems with it too: Mesters himself is clearly aware of the dangers of an undisciplined claim to inspiration. But the moral for the preacher is straightforward. The members of the congregation are not fools – and some of them may be saints. The multicoloured wisdom of God (Eph. 3.10) still shows itself through the members of the Church. Preachers need to take St Paul's questions to heart: 'Did the word of God originate with you? Or are you the only people it has reached?' (1 Cor. 14.36).

3 Learning from the congregation

Sobered by this thought, we might ask how we can engage more constructively with the congregation, and make best use of what they have to offer. First, it would seem sensible to work with them in the creation of the sermon. No one person can possibly have access to all the best illustrations or examples. Of necessity, his or her life experience is restricted and will reflect a specific context. The congregation, on the other hand, corporately possesses a vast range of life experiences, which provide a well from which the preacher can draw. The congregation can put flesh on the nature of the problems which face ordinary Christians living in the world, they can share accounts of times when faith was difficult or times when God felt close. How does God speak to people? What examples of providential care or guidance are out there to be used?

Instances and illustrations which do not reflect the preacher's gender, age, class or experience, but which supplement and complement them, can be incorporated into the sermon.

This process need not be excessively time-consuming or exhausting. Half a dozen people can provide a mass of material which can be used anonymously and sensitively to earth many different sermons. Of course, I am not suggesting that confidences may be broken, or secrets publicised from the pulpit. But I do remember asking a lifelong Christian what the Trinity meant to her and receiving the answer, 'Not a lot'. It gave me the start of a sermon and a point of departure. I asked a different set of people about the way in which they pictured God, and was privileged to be given a range of unusual images that I could never have thought of from within myself. Members of the congregation can help the preacher ground the message in all the variety of real life. Then it will ring true and speak to many more people than a sermon which has come solely out of one person's experience.

4   Giving answers or raising questions?

It is more difficult to arrange for involvement in the actual sermon. Black congregations seem to find it natural to exhort and encourage the preacher. 'Come up higher!'; 'Make it plain'; 'A-men!' (or if the preacher is labouring, 'Help him, Jesus'!) – these give the preacher instant feedback and encouragement. But even in a different subculture it might be possible to structure the sermon in such a way as to stimulate active engagement with the subject matter. Can the material be shaped so as to *raise* problems as well as solve them? Is it possible to show the congregation some of our working: how we came to this or that conclusion, why we made that decision? Some of the most effective sermons I've heard appear to share the process of construction as a continuing conversation with the text and the congregation. Can we ask real questions and not just rhetorical ones? Walter Hollenweger has characterized Jesus as 'the dialogic Christ' because he was always engaging people in dialogue. Jesus challenged assumptions, posed questions and presented alternatives which compelled decision. The conventional sermon will not permit very much, if any, public dialogue, but can it replicate something of the 'feel' of a dialogue? Passivity is encouraged when the preacher brings a message all buttoned up, with answers to every question anyone could ever think of. A preacher who clearly presumes that the congregation is thinking as they listen will discourage an attitude of uncritical acceptance. All this emphasizes the importance of those church members who can be relied upon not to toe the party line. Every church contains those who will produce the idiosyncratic insight, the observation which doesn't fit and which challenges the cosy world, those people who are prepared to say, 'It does not seem so to me'. Such awkward customers, like new Christians, are precious to the preacher, since they have not yet learned what may not be said.

5   Encouraging feedback

My last suggestion concerns the post-sermon phase. Is it possible to enlist the congregation's help after the sermon has been preached? Congregations are seldom totally silent at the church door. 'Lovely sermon, vicar', is a form of feedback – but it may be an example of good manners overriding honesty and, in any case, it fails to pick up those who found the sermon unendurable but who do not wish to offend or hurt. Moreover, this kind of feedback sets evaluation firmly in the mould of assessment. The sermon is marked as if it were a performance at the world figure-skating championships. If you are lucky, you get 5.5; if not, it's another string of 3.4s. But neither the elation nor the gloom which follow are especially constructive.

There is a different type of evaluation which focuses on description and is rather more useful. Here, liking or not liking is a minor issue: instead, the person evaluating the sermon concentrates on describing what it was about and the effect it had on him or her. As someone describes the sermon which he or she heard, the preacher is able to form a much clearer idea of its strengths and weaknesses *as preached*. After all, in this situation the hearer is always right. If they did not pick up your moving story about the dying dog, then something went wrong either with the construction of that section or in the way it was delivered. (Alternative explanations such as, 'They are an evil and adulterous generation', are possible but should be used only when you are desperate.) Questions which ask for description will give the preacher hard evidence about what was communicated. What was the subject of the sermon? What parts can you remember? Were there any stories in it? What effect did it have on you? What did you take away from it? The answers to these questions may plunge the preacher into despair – but on the whole, people will not know that they are having that effect. After all, they are not being asked whether or not they liked it, just about what they remember of it.

It is encouraging to read that this kind of feedback is becoming more popular. Roger Van Harn, for example, has instituted a system of diaries for 'sermon listeners' where about four people at a time agree to keep diaries which will provide him, among other things, with comment on his sermons.[7] A group of people who are prepared, for just three or four sermons, to respond in this way are worth any number of congratulatory handshakes at the door. In fact, if you can find just one person who will honestly and objectively comment on your preaching in the descriptive mode, then clasp them to you and never let them go.

THE PREACHER'S ROLE

This chapter has tried to sketch some of the subtle forces at work in what is quite clearly a power situation. One person speaks – and 40, or 400, listen. The imbalance raises interesting questions. But the situation does not have to be one where anyone is restricted or infantilized. Christ calls us to freedom and to maturity. The picture of the preacher as parent 'chewing up the morsels' does not appeal to me – but nor does that of the preacher speaking only 'smooth words', for fear of the people. I prefer to work with two other images, both of which, in their different ways, show that the preacher comes out from among the congregation and listens and works with them.

The first is from Carlos Mesters. He considers two contrasting roles for the preacher – the stork and the midwife. The stork, somewhat in the style of the conventional preacher, 'presents the child to the parents – as if the child came from outside the parents, as if there is no need for gestation and painful birth. The midwife helps in the painful birthing of the child who has been gestating in the mother's womb.'[8]

The second image is borrowed from Thomas Long. He depicts

the preacher as an explorer of a deep and mysterious cave who, after much toil, finally stands awe-struck before some breathtaking subterranean sight:

> Then, knowing what he must do, he carefully retraces his path, scrambles to the mouth of the cave, and with the dirt of the journey still on his face and his flashlight waving excitedly, he calls to those who have been waiting on him, 'Come on, have I got something to show you!'[9]

12 The word-processor in the pew

The previous chapter was concerned with what happens to the balance of power when an individual addresses a group. For the purposes of the exercise, it made sense to regard the congregation as one whole, whether they numbered four or four hundred. However, in many respects the congregation is not an entity. It is often more useful to look at them as a collection of individuals, even when there are only two or three gathered together. In fact, even very small congregations are not monochrome. The people who make them up are a diverse bunch, different in background, life experience, understanding of the faith, gender, social class and present situation. They are a mixed-ability class – and a challenge for any teacher.

This helps to account for that strange and exasperating phenomenon, the misheard message. In theory, there are as many possible mishearings of your sermon as there are listeners:

> Something happens between the preacher's lips and the congregation's ears that is beyond prediction or explanation. The same sermon sounds entirely different at 9.00 and 11.15 am on a Sunday morning. Sermons that make me weep leave my listeners baffled, and sermons that seem cold to me find warm responses. Later in the week, someone quotes part of my sermon back to me, something she has found extremely meaningful – only I never said it.[1]

If we take the diversity of the congregation seriously, preaching looks slightly less sensible than trying to fill empty bottles by throwing a bucket of milk out of an upstairs window.

EARS TO HEAR?

Our hunches about the ability of the congregation to hear or mishear the sermon are confirmed when we turn to communication theory. For more than 50 years researchers in this field have emphasized the importance of what the listener brings – in fact, you cannot say that communication has taken place at all until the message has been received and processed by the hearers.

This axiom has been strangely slow to win acceptance in the Christian world. Charles Kraft has identified some of the common myths which run counter to it: 'The key to effective communication is the precise formulation of the message' (rough paraphrase: 'If you speak clearly everyone will understand you'); 'Words contain their meanings' ('We all know what "love" means then'); 'What people really need is more information' ('Why can't you understand me? I've said it nine times'); and so on.[2] Such sayings sound plausible. Communication theory has made them problematic.

We need to take seriously the facts that communication is not just a matter of sending information, that no meaning is received until the receiver has decoded the signal, that meanings are negotiated not transmitted, and that they are personal. The receiver decides what the message means, because the receiver interprets the world through a set of personal understandings and associations which give meaning to words and sentences.

Fortunately for the future of conversation, much of the time we share these understandings with the speaker, and there is enough common ground between our associations to make some kind of communication possible. In any case, communication is a percentage word: there's a continuum between blank incomprehension at one end and 'knowing even as also I am known' at the other. Just occasionally, we see what might happen if we had no shared stock of meanings. The phrase, 'It was hellish', can mean both 'It was terrible' and 'It was brilliant', depending on the age and home location of the speaker. The slogan, 'Jesus is well wicked,' indicates praise in some Christian circles. The message may be universal but it still has to be encoded in the phrases of a particular culture. If that culture is opaque to the receiver, the meaning will be distorted. Whether or not the message is clear depends on the capacity of the listener to make sense of it. More accurately, since the receiver will probably make some sense of it somehow, we ought to speak of clarity only when the listener has made roughly the same sense of the message as was intended by the speaker.

Just to complicate matters a little more, it is not just the meanings of words which cause confusion. Words also carry associations and emotions; they evoke loyalties and commitments. Nor do they arrive 'clean': they are coloured by the listener's prejudices and assumptions, and by the way in which the situation or the speaker is perceived. If some men can only 'hear' a female preacher as 'daughter' or 'mother', then they will have great difficulty in receiving the message without static. But that's not the preacher's fault.

It is also possible that in a media-saturated age people have developed the skill of screening out unwanted information. We are bombarded with messages, both aural and visual, many of which are personally draining and disturbing. As our senses reel under the assault we learn to tune out and switch off. But we do not leave this skill behind at the church door. As Wesley Carr has said, 'The old music hall gag, "I don't wish to know that. Kindly leave the stage", has become a sort of slogan for contemporary survival.'[3]

In much the same vein, Richard Ward has noted our capacity to employ selective inattention – that is, to set aside a single-focus, high-tension attention in favour of dropping in to one stimulus for a time, while being aware of but not wholly engaged by a number of others.[4] The television set may be on all evening, but no one watches it to the exclusion of casual conversation. The car radio is at one moment the centre of our attention, and a minute later just background noise. The screen shows pictures of a pop group while, at the same time, a stream of words moves from right to left across the bottom of the screen. Our age is not more intelligent than earlier generations; we are just more prepared to pick and mix at the sensory sweet counter.

So the congregation is diverse – diverse enough to hear one sermon in dozens of different ways. People are aware of what is said, while at times not giving it much attention; they filter what is said, giving it meaning according to individual understandings and emotional weight and colour according to individual preference and prejudice. They will include in their negotiation of meaning non-verbal or even irrelevant factors. Most of the time they will arrive at a meaning not dissimilar to what was intended; some of the time they will mishear in ways which will amuse, depress, exasperate or bewilder the preacher.

I do not believe that these considerations should leave us in despair. One famous orator was asked for three top tips on public speaking. He replied, 'Consider your audience, consider your audience, consider your audience.' Roger Van Harn has contrasted two sets of assumptions about preaching. One puts *preaching* at the centre, the other puts *hearing*. We need to consider this shift of emphasis. What will happen if we substitute, 'The minister listens and speaks a response in the sermon', for 'The minister speaks the sermon and listens for a response'; 'The minister finishes the sermon', for 'The congregation finishes the sermon'; 'The test of value lies in what is said', for 'The test of value lies in what is heard'?[5] It may be no bad thing for preachers to have to redress the traditional balance.

STRATEGIES FOR WORKING TOGETHER

If we want to take the congregation seriously as co-shapers of the sermon, what practical strategies might we use?

Remember the diversity of the congregation

There is a growing literature to help us to keep the diversity of the congregation in the forefront of our minds. Communication theory highlights the power of the receiver to shape the message. The work of Myers and Briggs on different personality preferences, of James Fowler on stages of faith, and of Deborah Tannen on the different ways in which men and women interpret conversational interchanges – all these remind us that we're speaking to individuals. Research on learning styles suggests that people have preferred ways of processing information. Novels and plays will help us live through, and experience vicariously, stages of life and rites of passage of which we may have no personal experience. This kind of reading is not to make us into mini experts on everything. At the heart is our willingness to listen, to use our imaginations and to try to empathize with people. There is a variety and richness in those whom we might be tempted to lump together as 'the congregation'.

Accept that God is sovereign in every life

In the end we sow the seed and God gives the increase. We need to take less thought for the harvest than for the proper sowing. I heard one eminent preacher, who was disconcertingly dismissive of his preaching, say, 'As I go up to the pulpit I increasingly find myself muttering "I believe in the Holy Spirit, the Lord, the giver of life"'. This is not just a piece of conventional piety. As we prepare the sermon we pray that God will use it; we thus accept that the Spirit will be at work independently of us. It may be enormously annoying to discover that we are not totally in control of everything that happens – but that experience will accentuate the sovereignty of the Spirit and the dignity of the hearers, and will keep us properly humble.

Admit that people are autonomous

Humility is the only sensible stance. We have to learn to let go of the sermon, and accept that we cannot stuff people with God's word independently of their willingness to give it room. Walter Brueggemann likens the process to therapy:

> As every therapist knows, finally only the other party in the conversation can decide to what extent new insight is permitted to subvert, and in what way. Thus the text and the preacher provide the materials for subversion, but the permission to subvert belongs to the hearer of the text. That is why, in my judgement, one can fund subversive imagination, but we do not preempt from others the act of imagination.[6]

Try to create a sense of expectancy

Preaching stands a better chance of being heard when the congregation is actively listening for God to speak. This openness to God depends largely on the individual church member – but nevertheless the preacher can play some part in creating the willingness to listen. The sermon can remind people that there may be a word from God among the many words which the preacher will speak. Often enough, congregations settle down with no expectation of being addressed by

God, no sense that this might be a critical moment, that today might be the day when the words catch fire and the bush burns. Sometimes the eyes close, or at least glaze over, before the preacher has even begun. I remember thinking at the beginning of one sermon, 'Give me a break, madam, I've not started yet. At least allow me two minutes in which to be boring.' The preacher can openly signal the possibility that God might have something important to say this morning and that he might say it within the next 15 minutes. In a fascinating study of the preaching of Billy Graham, Mark Greene notes Graham's habit of referring early on in the sermon to the invitation to come forward. Most people who attend Graham's meetings already know that the invitation will be made at the end – but he still thinks it important to signal the possibility of explicit response well in advance.[7]

Take the trouble to get to know the congregation

It is only honest to accept that some preaching which does not communicate may be the result of our failure to take account of the world views – the values, the culture and personal situations of the members of the congregation. Some mishearings may mark a failure of empathy, pastoral care or enquiry on our part.

Our research needs to focus on four areas.

1   SITTING WHERE THEY SIT

This phrase is often used as a metaphor, but I use it here in its literal sense. As part of the process of focusing on the listener, it is helpful to sit in different places in the church and ask yourself the question, 'What will the person sitting in this seat see and hear?' Richard Ward claims that this was John Wesley's practice.[8] Certainly, the strategy will concentrate our thoughts on the individual – especially if you pray for the person who will occupy that seat.

2   LEARNING ABOUT THE AREA

For all their differences, the individual members will share much of the culture of the region. It is time well spent to undertake an amateur social and cultural audit, to discover how people spend their leisure time, who are the big employers (or how much unemployment there is in the area), who are the local heroes, what are the popular night spots, and the folk myths. It did not take much research to find out, in one North East town, that the greatest compliment you could pay the new curate was to say, 'He's a good eater', that the Jarrow march was not dead history, and that Kevin Keegan walked on water. This is a process which McElvaney calls 'taking the pulse of the saints': 'Spend some time with Austa Wyrick, the 86-year-old across the street from the parsonage. Seek out Charlie Sims on the courthouse square. Have a hamburger at Presto's Dairy Queen so you can absorb some wisdom from Presto, the blind proprietor.'[9]

3 FEEDING THE IMAGINATION

The congregation can be divided into categories, despite the dangers of stereotyping. In fact, stereotyping is not a wholly negative process. Lewis Higdon lists the following groups to be found in most churches: young people, the elderly, the angry, friendly folk, the frail, families, the faithful, the fearful, doubting Thomases, loners and visitors.[10] The value of this list is that it encourages us to picture these groups in our imaginations. What does the world look and feel like to this type of person? What are their hopes, fears, stresses, joys and pains? How will they hear my sermon? By so doing, we do not pretend that we are really entering the mind of any individual by a mystical process of intuition. However, we can claim to be developing our capacity to see the world a little more as they see it, to flesh out the category, and thereby to give the individuals within that category a face and a voice, even while accepting that each person is unique.

A similar exercise is advocated by Fred Craddock – you might like to try this. He suggests that you take a blank sheet of paper and write at the top, 'What's it like to be?' Underneath we write a phrase 'descriptive of one concrete facet of human experience'. This might be 'facing surgery', 'living alone', 'fired from one's position', '14 years old'. 'For the next 15 minutes scribble on the page every thought, recollection, feeling, experience, name, place, sound, smell, or taste that comes to mind.' He suggests that this kind of exercise will result in a 'reduction in the number of sermons that either make no contact with the listener or make contact in ways unintended and often counterproductive.'[11]

This is one of the most obvious ways of ensuring that the sermon touches the real lives of individuals. Most of us acquire a vast store of information about members of the congregation. This has nothing to do with tittle-tattle or gossip; much of it comes through the ordinary interactions of friendship, some of it through pastoral encounters. We are not speaking of the preacher, in Craddock's phrase, 'as vacuum cleaner', sucking up personal trifles in order to embarrass people from the pulpit by our indiscreet use of confidential information. Whatever we use will be impenetrably disguised. And most of it will not be especially confidential. St Paul seems to have set great store on the public exchange of news. It is one of the ways in which our preaching can be relevant and informed.

IN THEIR SHOES

The theme of this chapter is that whatever we say will be customized and processed by the individual. We have a responsibility to ensure that each person is helped rather than hindered to hear the specific word which God wants to speak to them.

Below is a sermon on the text, 'Blessed are the meek'. It is shorter than usual because it was written for a television meditation. After it, you will find an exercise which brings together many of the issues discussed above.

> The meek are supposed to inherit the earth, though the graffiti says, 'If that's OK with the rest of you.' We are more used to Robocop and Terminator inheriting the earth. Blessed are the pushy for they get their own way, and people do what they say even while they hate them. Mr Nice Guy wins the wimp of the year award. You don't find the meek driving up your exhaust at 70 mph flashing their lights and sounding the horn. Nor do the meek cut you up at roundabouts and scream off into the distance with a casual two-finger salute. It looks as if the best way to live is to throw your weight about. After all, money talks, God is on the side of the big battalions, every man has his price ... and so on. Not exactly Patience Strong is it? As rugby coaches say, 'Get your retaliation in first'.

And yet … I'm aware that Jesus said the meek will possess the earth. And that he described himself as meek. And Moses was meek. We're not talking about doormats here. Our ideas of meekness will have to change. Meek and mild, won't say boo to a goose, won't fit.

A few years ago I watched an eight-stone young woman throwing six-foot males over her shoulder. She had represented Great Britain at judo of course. That did give her a slight advantage. Judo is the gentle or meek way. In apparent weakness, in yielding, in using the weight, power and aggression of the opponent, the expert turns the world upside-down. Those who fly through the air have an opportunity to meditate on the truth of strength through weakness.

The car park of a church I used to go to was tarmacked. It looked a solid job. But come the Spring and daffodils forced their way up through the tarmac. I thought we ought to have put up a notice: 'God rules OK'.

The meek people have learned, sometimes the hard way, that God's power works through those who are open to it, those who don't make a song and dance but draw on that inexhaustible supply. The meek are gentle but like tempered steel. They may seem a pushover, but because their resources are in God and not in themselves they can often display extraordinary courage, strength and persistence. As a boy I read the story of Toyohiko Kagawa, a Japanese Christian who went to live alongside people in the slums of Shinkawa. He was often ridiculed and sometimes attacked. And when that happened, he used to run away. I really liked the sound of this man! Doormat. But the next day he would come back again. And he went on like that indefinitely – on and on and on, like an Ariston advert.

Our kitchen ceiling is a mess. It nearly came down because there was a leak in the bathroom above it. It was only a small leak. But it nearly brought the ceiling down. I don't think we'd fully appreciated that behind each drop of water were the total resources of the Kielder Dam.

Imagine how this sermon will be heard by:

1 someone recently bereaved;

2 a teenager who is being ridiculed at school;

3 someone who has little connection with the Church and who has switched on by accident;

4 a parent worried about his or her children.

Write a short paragraph for each character. You might like to make notes or write in the form of a stream of consciousness. Note their reactions to each move of the sermon. Where does the sermon touch them and come alive? Where is it irrelevant? You have a limitless number of options since we don't actually know very much about any of them! The exercise is really about imagining ourselves in someone else's shoes. If the task seems artificial or difficult, then substitute someone whose situation you do know.

Now make one alteration to the sermon for each character (four in all). These changes can be additions or subtractions but they should make the message relate more closely to each character.

13 Playing squash against a haystack

Donald Coggan tells a story about 'a theological student who wrote out a sermon for his homiletics teacher, and read it to him. A long silence ensued, and the student sensed that there was something ominous about it. At last he could wait no longer: 'Will it do, sir?' he said, 'Will it do?' '*Do what?*' was the reply.'[1]

What are sermons good for? All over the world parents have wonderful ways of putting their children down. One of my favourites is the sceptical question: 'What difference is that going to make to the price of fish in Grimsby?' Much is claimed for sermons – but do they deliver the goods? Fine words perhaps, but in the end, will they butter the parsnips?

Preaching is an attempt to change things. To be more precise, to change people. So, preaching tries to *do* something:

> The purpose of preaching is transformation. We undertake theater that is potentially life-changing. This is the meeting. This is where the transformative action takes place. This is not talk about some other meeting some-where else. This dramatic moment intends that folk should go away changed, perhaps made whole, perhaps savaged.[2]

'Transformation' sets the stakes very high. What exactly does it mean? And how can we achieve it? We grant that preaching is a craft and that the sermon is a cunningly devised 15 minutes of persuasion. But transformation?

The claim doesn't seem likely. We hope that people will hear what we say and take it further, by applying it to themselves in a personal way or by seeing implications, ramifications and depths which we did not spot. Depressingly, we notice how thoroughly they process the messages they receive. They filter them through their present understandings, their prejudices, hopes, interests, fears, past experiences, expectations, even their hearing aids. All too often we find that they have applied them to someone else ('Wonderful sermon Vicar, every part of it was right for somebody in this church'). Or perhaps they have failed to see that it was relevant at all. When we discover that they have forgotten even the main point by lunch time, isn't time to call it a day? Transformation?

And yet sometimes we preach and seem to be putting into words what people feel or hope almost before they themselves realize it. Sometimes we speak *for* people. The atmosphere is electric. And the result in the listeners is something akin to gratitude. 'I didn't know that was what was I was feeling until you said it. Now I understand.'

This was one of the great gifts of Martin Luther King. Listen to him in the energy of his youth, at the beginning of a new day for African Americans. His congregation is *tired*. Luther King takes up the feeling and gives it meaning:

> You know, my friends, there comes a time when people get *tired*
> Of being trampled over by the iron feet of oppression. (*Thundering applause*)
> There comes a time my friends when people get *tired*
> Of being flung across the abyss of humiliation where they experience the bleakness of nagging despair. (*Keep talking!*)
> There comes a time when people get *tired*
> Of being pushed out of the glittering sunlight of life's July and left standing amidst the piercing chill of an Alpine November. (*Three minutes of tumult*)[3]

Three minutes of tumult may not be a common occurrence at Evensong, but any preacher who can give people a new perspective and help them find a voice is changing lives. Don't knock it.

HOW DO SERMONS WORK?

When I watch an advertisement on television, I realize that I am being got at. The idea is that I should spend money on the product.

But television advertisements use a variety of techniques to effect that single aim – from crude ear-bending to subtle and allusive mini-soaps. Preaching takes place in an analogous situation: it is persuasive talk, it aims to change minds and hearts and, in particular, to evoke worship and repentance. It may attempt to achieve that purpose by direct attack or use more indirect means, like image or story.

I can illustrate this distinction from the sermons I collected. Among direct techniques I would include comments like these:

'Over there is the bookstall. You will find commentaries on all the books in the Bible. Perhaps now's the time to go across there and pluck one out.'

'And in the next few weeks we'll have a few excellent opportunities to invite those who do not usually attend church to do that: for the crib service here in two weeks time, or the High Street carol service a few days later, or for the Christingle.'

'How, as people of faith, do we live? Do we let go and let God do his thing in us and with us, or do we hang on for grim death?'

'I hope that all of us will have a similar Divine discontent.'

'As we celebrate Christmas we should be able to declare, "I do believe it". Thus we can try to live up to our Christian faith by becoming the Holy Family here.'

'Let not our generation ever forget those heady days.'

'May we never be too proud to ask.'

'So as we wait this Christmas Eve in eager anticipation of the celebration of Christmas Day, let us also live in the sure and certain hope of heaven.'

'Don't lie; don't let the sun go down on your anger; don't be horrible about people; don't be bitter, angry or fight; don't be sexually immoral; don't be greedy; don't be obscene.'

139

There are a number of techniques involved here – the challenging question, exhortation, both implied and explicit, direct commands, specific prescriptions. They all have their place. They nail the point down. Alongside them, however, there are other strategies of persuasion, where the method is less conspicuous and possibly more effective.

For example, sometimes it is enough to offer specific examples of the kind of action which might be appropriate at any time:

> To hunger and thirst after righteousness could mean taking part in the current demonstrations to do with the veal calves (as long as people stay within the law); it could mean writing to the bus company asking why the X22 at 8.45 is now a minibus rather than a long single-decker, it could mean verbalizing our disagreement with the 1 per cent payrise for nurses, while chairmen of companies are getting 75 per cent.

Very often the image will work more powerfully than direct exhortation:

> There is an artist in America who works with the leftovers thrown away at the rubbish dump – a bicycle wheel here, a cushion from a chair there – and creates beautiful things. So it is with God. He takes our leftovers and creates something wonderful.
>
> About four or five years ago Israel had one of the coldest and wettest winters ever. There was snow in the wilderness. And when the Spring came people saw flowers in the desert which hadn't been seen for 20 or 30 years. They had been there all that time waiting for the life-giving touch of water. O Thou Lord of life, send my roots rain.

This is a useful point at which to take one or two of your own sermons and analyse them, looking at four questions:

- What specifically were you hoping to *do* to the congregation?
- What would have counted as success?
- What techniques or strategies did you use in order to effect change?
- Which of these techniques would you rank as 'direct' and which as 'indirect'?

I hope the language of the exercise doesn't sound crude. By talking of 'doing' something to the congregation I am trying to sharpen the point that preaching aims to change people; it is not a few jolly observations strung together to fill 15 minutes. Nor am I implying that technique alone produces any worthwhile change. Spiritual change is the result of the activity of the Spirit. Nevertheless, it is always worth trying to understand more clearly what methods we do use, and how we expect them to change people.

I hope, after doing this exercise, that you can clearly see that change is normally expected to follow the sermon – though the form that change may take is diverse and not always immediately obvious (I certainly don't just mean activity or busyness). You have probably also identified a wide variety of techniques – a personal testimony, a clever analogy, an allusion to a biblical passage or a ringing affirmation of some profound truth. What exactly was the function of that story? And that purple passage – how was it intended to work? Was it supposed to illuminate the mind, warm the heart or stir the will? Or all three at once? These questions are designed to encourage you to look at the rhetoric of your sermons. Rhetoric is not a dirty word. It does not equal manipulation and is not an insult to God. Those who think that their sermons contain no rhetoric are either being disingenuous or are natural rhetoricians. Jesus himself appears to have used dozens of different techniques, and carefully crafted what he wanted to say.

How exactly do sermons hope to change people? I suggest three primary ways of effecting change.

1   BUYING INTO THE PACKAGE

What strikes me most forcibly about most sermons is that, in one way or another, they work by introducing the congregation to that total vision of the world which is the Christian faith. People are invited to buy into the Christian package. Though the methods vary, each sermon appeals to an element within the circle. A highly specific injunction, 'Get a book about the Bible from the church bookstall', is connected to views about the importance of the Bible for knowing who God is, how the world works and what it means to be a disciple. The invitation to live within a metaphor, 'Advent is about standing in God's queue', is stitched into a complex of ideas – prayer, reflection and waiting on God, God's loving care of the Christian, a God of surprises, and so on. The network of concepts, assumptions, authorities, models, commands, values, lifestyles, is a tightly constructed whole, which may be accessed at any point.

All of which suggests that sermons work by making the whole Christian world view attractive, by bringing people into it, helping them stay within it and encouraging them to live in harmony with its ethos. Sermons create a world, maintain a world and explicate a world. They succeed to the extent to which people are incorporated into that world. Richard Lischer argues that preaching *forms* a community of faith over time. In a discussion of storytelling and illustrations, he maintains:

> But the church is not saved by stories but by the God who is rendered by them and emerges by their means. Our God has but a single story. Its most important purpose is neither identification nor illustration (of some other truth?) but *incorporation*.'[4]

2   THE THREEFOLD APPEAL

A second critical factor in effecting change concerns the preferred preaching style of the regular preacher. By this I assume that most preachers have their own style into which they slip naturally. At the risk of caricature, some sermons, or parts of sermons, typically say, 'See life this way'; some say, 'Feel this in your heart'; yet others say, 'This is what you must do'. It is important not to get stuck in one style. Over time, I believe sermons ought to speak to the mind, the heart and the will.

An appeal to the mind is effective in so far as it offers the listener a coherent view of life. Sermons probably aren't a very good way of teaching somebody; and 'poor, talkative Christianity' has always suffered from an excess of words. Nevertheless, sermons can clarify ideas, explain doctrines and tease out implications. They can show how the various pieces of experience fit together and deal with those aspects of life (like suffering) which appear difficult to contain within the circle. They can baptize 'secular' experience into Christ.

But equally, sermons can warm the heart. An appeal to the heart aims to inspire warmth, longing for God, devotion and worship. Pulpit oratory is less fashionable than it used to be, and the synthetic emotionalism of the televangelist is to be shunned – but if preachers speak of the love of God in Christ we must expect that people's hearts will be touched. In fact, something has gone wrong if they are not.

Sermons can also move the will. An appeal to the will hopes to inspire action, service, commitment, obedience to Christ, and the ability to express a vision of the world in a practical Christian lifestyle. Here, the power of imagination cannot be underestimated. An image, an instance, or a story which shows what reality could be like, can carry an electrifying charge. As a result of seeing possibilities, someone decides that they will join a Lent group, or buy a book or apologize to their friend. A sermon can initiate practical change.

Now it is worth asking if your normal style favours one approach against the other two. If it does, you run the risk of distortion and lack of balance. For example, an exclusive appeal to the mind may produce a dry and overintellectualized Christianity. It is not enough to say, 'People are changed by being exposed to biblical truth'. Doctrinal exposition alone will not do the trick. If the appeal is exclusively to the intellect, it will lack the crucial electrical charge. On the other hand, a style which only addresses the heart may result in soft-centred discipleship, warm and fuzzy but lacking in practical action or coherent belief. Again, being urged to mend one's ways can feel like being told to eat up your greens. A little good advice goes a long way, and exhortations are often answered

143

rudely in the privacy of one's thoughts. 'So let us all resolve ...' ('I might, or there again, I might not.') 'Don't you sometimes ...?' ('Mind your own business!') Exhortations to action need to be tied into devotion to Christ, and an understanding of the mighty acts of redemption.

The need for this kind of balance has long been recognized. A colleague of mine was told, 'Let him jump up and down till what's in his head gets down to his heart'. Neglect of the practical invites the old charge, 'So heavenly minded that he's no earthly use'. A wayside pulpit motto emphasizes the importance of devotion, 'Too busy to pray is too busy'.

3   WHIZZ-BANG AND DRIP-DRIP

My third observation returns to the idea of transformation. It seems to me that transformation can come in either of two ways. It can be a matter of an instant, when the preached word burns in the heart, breaks down the barriers and creates a new world instantaneously. The Chinese proverb, 'When the disciple is ready the teacher comes', is a way of assuring us that when the tree is ready to fall it only needs the slightest breath to bring it down. Preaching in such a situation is a humbling experience. It seems as if almost anything I say will work a miracle. We hope for this effect, pray for it and prepare for it – but we cannot organize it. Charles Williams put it this way: 'We build the altar here so that the fire may fall over there'. This means that we must never give up on the possibility that such a cataclysmic change can take place, and may take place next time we preach. This very morning might find someone on the road to Damascus.

On the other hand, when we speak of transformation, we need not imply sudden or cataclysmic change. The road to Emmaus is as common as the road to Damascus. To take an analogy, transformation by television is seldom a matter of one or two programmes. Our attitudes and values are changed imperceptibly by exposure to the medium and its characteristic way of communicating, as much as by our viewing on any given evening. So with the sermon. Perhaps it doesn't matter much if people can't remember the headings of the sermon at lunch time. Perhaps sermons don't work like that. Perhaps sermons work, like television (and like liturgy?), because they gradually change the way people see the world. Slowly they woo people away from one picture of the world and open them up to being captivated by a different one.

Brueggemann likens this process to that of therapy. For him, transformation is 'the slow, steady process of inviting people into a counterstory about God, world, neighbour and self' – a story which gradually subverts the hold that other stories have upon them. 'The new world is not given whole, any more than the new self is given abruptly in psychotherapy. It is given only a little at a time, one text at a time, one miracle at a time, one poem, one healing, one pronouncement, one promise, one commandment.'[5]

All this is enormously encouraging to any preacher – especially to one who has to address the same congregation week by week – because it suggests that sermons work in ways which we recognize as being related to ordinary life. Preachers don't have to stagger under the burden of producing total transformations of life in the congregation every time they preach. Everyone would probably get overtired. Hearing a sermon is something like having lunch: it does you good but you can't always remember what you ate, particularly last Thursday week. So if the hearers forget large parts of sermons, or even whole sermons, does it matter all that much? Like Holy Communion, the word faithfully preached will do its work – even if the congregation can't remember every detail later.

I believe this thought will help us in the matter of originality. Much of what we preach will be familiar, the way brown bread, butter and Cheddar cheese is familiar. From a communications perspective, John Bluck offers reassurance: 'At least half the content of any communication event is redundant ... serving only to make and keep contact between sender and receiver, to keep the channels open and the "show on the road".'[6] Most church liturgy (even of those churches which claim not to have a formal liturgy) and a high proportion of sermons are redundant in this sense. They say nothing new or unexpected, but serve to reassure and keep the tradition going (though we hope that each time a congregation hears the old, old story they will enter into it once again). It is fascinating to discover that Martin Luther King was reared in a tradition in which preachers felt free to preach purple passages many times over. Large parts of Luther King's most memorable sermons were made up of sections that had been honed by frequent repetition. Like a singer who is greeted with rapturous applause after only one or two notes of a well-loved song, Luther King was able to rely on the congregation's recognizing and applauding the familiar words. But why ever not? Our culture expects each sermon to be newly minted. But we do not complain that *Hamlet* was the same as last time, or that Mozart's *Requiem* contains no new notes. Though it is pointless, in one sense, to try to transpose the culture of the theatre or the concert or a Black congregation into a different setting, we can still recognize that a necessary part of transformation involves saying nothing new or unexpected, but means reassuring people and keeping the tradition going.

None of this implies that any old words will do on the grounds that congregations forget most of what they hear anyway. No doubt God can work miracles in any way he chooses. I have heard of someone who was converted by reading a genealogy – though I lack the details and, as a strategy, it doesn't seem a very sturdy basket into which to put all one's homiletical eggs. Familiar truth doesn't have to be wrapped in words which are banal, trite, or well-worn just to make sure that God has a higher fence to jump. The preacher is still under an obligation to try to say the same old things in new ways, and to struggle to find words which are true and at the same time arresting, interesting and insightful.

I don't want the last word to be about words, however. It is right to look at rhetoric and try to understand how sermons might produce change in those who listen to them. But rhetoric must serve the Gospel, and must always treat the hearers with dignity and respect. More important than any technique must be the congregation's sense that the one who speaks to them speaks out of the authority of first-hand experience. As a friend of mind puts it, 'They must feel that he or she has been to the wire'. There is something about realizing that the preacher has touched the rock which communicates instantly. Pain speaks to pain; honesty touches the nerve; wrestling with God leaves a mark on the preacher – and thence on the congregation. Here is one for whom these are matters of life and death. In a penetrating passage Hans van der Geest says, 'I will awaken deep experiences in others to the extent that I am able to reach myself ... If I rationalize a pious faith in order to agree with a theological theory, then I am closing myself off, and in the worship service I am drawing from a well which is going dry'.[7]

The hope of the sermon lies in the authenticity of the preacher, and the authenticity of the preacher lies in the encounter with the living God.

References

Introduction

1   Burghardt, Walter J., *Preaching: the Art and the Craft*, New York/Mahwah, Paulist Press, 1987, p.45.
2   Cited in Burghardt, op. cit., p.45.

1   The passage, the whole passage and nothing but the passage

1   For an exciting example of one person's experimental reading, see Walter Moberly's 'Proclaiming Christ crucified: some reflections on the use and abuse of the gospels', in *Anvil*, Vol. 5, No. 1, 1988, pp.31–52.

3   What's cooking?

1   Quoted in Thielicke, Helmut, *Encounter with Spurgeon*, James Clarke, 1964.
2   Burghardt, Walter J., *Preaching: the Art and the Craft*, New York/Marwah, Paulist Press, 1987, pp.115–16.
3   Adam, Peter, *Speaking God's Words: a Practical Theology of Preaching*, Leicester, InterVarsity Press, 1996, p.131.
4   Robinson, Haddon, *Biblical Preaching*, Grand Rapids, Michigan, Baker Book House, 1980, pp.79ff.
5   Camery Hoggatt, Jerry, *Speaking of God*, Peabody, Massachusetts, Hendrickson, 1995.

4 Curbing a frisky theology

1   Long, Thomas, 'The use of Scripture in contemporary preaching', in *Interpretation*, Vol. 44, No. 4, 1990, p.347.
2   op. cit., p.347.

5 Is it good news?

1   Motl, J., 'Homiletics and integrating the seminary curriculum' in *Worship* Vol. 64, No. 1, January 1990, pp.24–30.
2   Lorenzen, Thorwald, 'Responsible preaching' in *Scottish Journal of Theology*, Vol. 33, No. 5, October 1980, pp.453–69.
3   Troeger, Thomas, 'Emerging new standards in the evaluation of effective preaching', in *Worship*, Vol. 64, No. 4, July 1990, pp.290–307, especially pp.299–300.

6 Learning from the experts

1   Wood, Victoria, *Barmy*, London, Methuen, 1987, p.53.
2   Middleton, Christopher, 'Speakers cornered', *Weekend Telegraph*, 12 November 1994.
3   Wood, Victoria, op. cit., p.26.
4   Troeger, Thomas, *Imagining a Sermon*, Nashville, Abingdon Press, 1990, p.40.
5   Troeger, op. cit., p.45.

7 The shapely sermon

1   Hamilton, Donald, *Homiletical Handbook*, Nashville, Broadman Press, 1992.
2   Williams, Rowan, *Open to Judgement*, London, Darton, Longman and Todd, 1994, pp.64–6.
3   Cotes, Mary, 'Standing in the stable', in Heather Walton and Susan Durber (eds), *Silence in Heaven*, London, SCM Press, 1994, pp.4–8.
4.   Lowry, Eugene, *How to Preach a Parable*, Nashville, Abingdon, 1989.
5   Lowry, Eugene, *The Homiletical Plot*, Atlanta, John Knox Press, 1980, p.25.

8   Faith, hope and clarity

1   Burns, Robert, 'Rantin' Ravin' Rabbie', in *Holy Fair*.
2   Kounin, J. S., *Discipline and Group Management in Classrooms*, New York, Holt, Rinehart and Winston, 1970.
3   Streeter, David, 'Paul and the doctrine of justification by faith, Part 2', in *Crossway*, Autumn 1993, pp.4–5.

9   The eggstain on the waistcoat

1   Craddock, Fred B., *Preaching*, Nashville, Tennessee, Abingdon Press, 1985, p.196.
2   Cotes, Mary, 'Standing in the stable', in Heather Walton and Susan Durber (eds), *Silence in Heaven*, London, SCM Press, 1994, pp.4–8.
3   Brueggemann, Walter, *The Bible and Postmodern Imagination*, London, SCM Press, 1993, pp.24–5.

10   A funny thing happened to me ...

1   Lischer, Richard, 'Preaching as the church's language', in *Listening to the Word: Studies in Honour of Fred B. Craddock*, Gail R. O'Day and Thomas G. Long (eds), Nashville, Abingdon Press, 1993, p.124.
2   Taylor, John V., *A Matter of Life and Death*, London, SCM Press, 1986, p.35.

11   Six feet above contradiction?

1   Calvin, John, 'Sermons on Timothy and Titus', Edinburgh, Banner of Truth, 1983, p. 945, quoted in Peter Adam, *Speaking God's Words*, Leicester, InterVarsity Press, 1996, p.141.
2   Norrington, David C., *To Preach or not to Preach?*, Carlisle, Paternoster Press, 1996.
3   Witten, Marsha G., *All is Forgiven: the Secular Message in American Protestantism*, New Jersey, Princeton University Press, 1993.
4   Witten, op. cit. p.82.
5   Mesters, Carlos, *Defenceless Flower*, New York, Orbis Books, 1989.

6   Mesters, op. cit., p.55.
7   Van Harn, Roger E., *Pew Rights*, Grand Rapids, Eerdmans, 1992, pp.155–8.
8   Mesters, op. cit., p.133.
9   Long, Thomas, 'The distance we have travelled: changing trends in preaching', in *Reformed Liturgy and Music*, Vol. 17, Winter 1983, p.14.

12   The word-processor in the pew

1   Brown Taylor, Barbara, *The Preaching Life*, Cambridge, Boston, Mass., Cowley Publications, 1993, p.85.
2   Kraft, Charles H., *Communication Theory for Christian Witness*, Nashville, Abingdon, 1983, pp.36ff.
3   Carr, Wesley, *Ministry and the Media*, London, SPCK, 1990, p.26.
4   Ward, Richard, *Speaking from the Heart*, Nashville, Tennessee, Abingdon, 1992, pp.121–4.
5   Van Harn, Roger, *Pew Rights*, Grand Rapids, Michigan, Eerdmans, 1992, p.14.
6   Brueggemann, Walter, *The Bible and Postmodern Imagination*, London, SCM, 1993, pp.90–91.
7   Greene, Mark, 'The Billy Graham global mission sermons: the power of belief', in *Vox Evangelica*, Vol. 26, October 1996, p.66.
8   Ward, op. cit., p.115.
9   McElvaney, William K., *Preaching from Camelot to Covenant*, Nashville, Abingdon Press, 1989, p.97.
10   Higdon, Lewis G., *Simply Preaching*, Norwich, Canterbury Press, 1995, pp.40–41.
11   Craddock, Fred B., *Preaching*, Nashville, Abingdon Press, 1985, pp.97–8.

13   Playing squash against a haystack

1   Coggan, Donald, *A New Day for Preaching*, London, SPCK, 1996, p.76.
2   Brueggemann, Walter, *The Bible and Postmodern Imagination*, London, SCM, 1993, p.24.
3   From Lischer, Richard, *The Preacher King: Martin Luther King Jr and the Word that Moved America*, New York, Oxford University

Press, 1995, p.87 (Lischer's annotations).

4   Lischer, Richard, *A Theology of Preaching*, Durham, N. Carolina, Labyrinth Press, 1993, p.90.

5   Brueggemann, op. cit., pp.24–5.

6   Bluck, John, *Christian Communication Reconsidered*, Geneva, World Council of Churches, 1989, p.23.

7   van der Geest, Hans, *Presence in the Pulpit: the Impact of Personality in Preaching*, trans. Douglas W. Stott, Atlanta, John Knox Press, 1981.